ISSUE 9, JULY 2020

AUSTRALIAN FOREIGN AFFAIRS

T0359130

Contributors

Anne-Marie Brady is a professor at the University of Canterbury and a global fellow at the Wilson Center in Washington, DC.

Nick Bisley is dean of humanities and social sciences and a professor of international relations at La Trobe University.

James Brown is a non-resident fellow at the United States Studies Centre and a former Australian Army officer.

Danielle Cave is deputy director of the International Cyber Policy Centre at the Australian Strategic Policy Institute.

Andrew Davies is a senior fellow at the Australian Strategic Policy Institute.

Kim McGrath is the author of *Crossing the Line: Australia's Secret History in the Timor Sea.*

Susan Harris Rimmer is Australian Research Council Future Fellow at Griffith Law School.

Max Walden is a reporter and producer at the ABC's Asia-Pacific newsroom.

Penny Wong is the shadow minister for foreign affairs and leader of the opposition in the Senate.

Australian Foreign Affairs is published three times a year by Schwartz Books Pty Ltd. Publisher: Morry Schwartz. ISBN 978-1-76064-2020 ISSN 2208-5912 ALL RIGHTS RESERVED. No part of this publication may be reproduced, stored in a retrieval system, or transmitted in any form by any means, electronic, mechanical, photocopying, recording or otherwise, without the prior consent of the publishers. Essays, reviews and correspondence © retained by the authors. Subscriptions – 1 year print & digital auto-renew (3 issues): $49.99 within Australia incl. GST. 1 year print and digital subscription (3 issues): $59.99 within Australia incl. GST. 2 year print & digital (6 issues): $114.99 within Australia incl. GST. 1 year digital only auto-renew: $29.99. Payment may be made by MasterCard, Visa or Amex, or by cheque made out to Schwartz Books Pty Ltd. Payment includes postage and handling. To subscribe, fill out the form inside this issue, subscribe online at www.australianforeignaffairs.com, email subscribe@australianforeignaffairs.com or phone 1800 077 514 / 61 3 9486 0288. Correspondence should be addressed to: The Editor, Australian Foreign Affairs, Level 1, 221 Drummond Street, Carlton VIC 3053 Australia Phone: 61 3 9486 0288 / Fax: 61 3 9486 0244 Email: enquiries@australianforeignaffairs.com Editor: Jonathan Pearlman. Deputy Editor: Julia Carlomagno. Associate Editor: Chris Feik. Consulting Editor: Allan Gyngell. Digital Editor and Marketing: Georgia Mill. Editorial Intern: Lachlan McIntosh. Management: Elisabeth Young. Subscriptions: Iryna Byelyayeva. Publicity: Anna Lensky. Design: Peter Long. Production Coordination: Marilyn de Castro. Typesetting: Akiko Chan. Cover photograph by Yuichiro Chino / Getty. Printed in Australia by McPherson's Printing Group.

SPY VS SPY

In February, Mike Burgess, the director-general of Australian Security Intelligence Organisation (ASIO), shared details of an elaborate espionage operation recently uncovered in Australia.

The operation, Burgess said, involved a sleeper agent who spent years in Australia establishing his cover and building community ties before being activated. The agent then began providing support to a network of spies who came to Australia, as well as relaying information to his handlers about dissident activities in Australia.

Burgess did not name the nation involved, though he would have known that his predecessor, Duncan Lewis, admitted to Peter Hartcher in the 2019 Quarterly Essay *Red Flag* that the main source of the "existential" threat posed by foreign espionage and interference was China.

Burgess's revelation about the presence of sophisticated sleeper cells in Australia may not be all that surprising, especially as such operations have long been a staple of spy novels, movies and television series. The more unexpected aspect was that he chose to reveal these details at all. He did so in Canberra when presenting ASIO's inaugural Annual Threat Assessment – a public statement that marks the latest step out of the shadows by Australia's intelligence agencies.

These days, Australia's domestic spy agency fields media inquiries, and its recent heads have delivered speeches and given press interviews. Australia's foreign collection agency, the Australian Secret Intelligence Service (ASIS), was kept secret – even from MPs – until the 1970s. But its former director-general, Nick Warner, delivered a public address in 2012, and its current head, Paul Symon, recently gave an interview to a podcast.

This decision to come out of the cold partly reflects these agencies' need to justify their growing funding and their increasing powers. In the past twenty years, Australia's intelligence spending has risen exponentially. In 2001, for instance, ASIO's budget was $61 million; this year it was $573 million. Meanwhile, changes in technology have given agencies enhanced potential to exercise surveillance, including over Australian citizens. The agencies evidently believe they need to both assure the public that these powers will not be misused and to build a case for receiving greater access to private communications and data.

But the need for public engagement also reflects the threats the nation's intelligence agencies now face. They are no longer primarily concerned with targeting foreign states or thwarting espionage by rival agencies, but with terrorism, foreign interference and cyber intrusions. Agents cannot simply stalk the halls of power in Canberra and Moscow. Instead, they must interact regularly with businesses, universities, community groups, and telecommunications and social media firms. Some of this will be undercover; much is not.

These trends, which are reshaping the role and focus of intelligence agencies, are only likely to accelerate. The COVID-19 pandemic has exacerbated tensions between China and the West, meaning that Australia will continue to be a target for China's vast network of spies. Already, according to Burgess, "There are more foreign intelligence officers and their proxies operating in Australia now than at the height of the Cold War." Spying is on the rise, and new technologies are enhancing the data collection and analysis capabilities of Australian agencies and their adversaries.

As these threats evolve, and intelligence agencies enter the public sphere, it will be crucial for citizens to understand the work they do. Just as with any other arm of government, we must ensure that they are fulfilling their main task – protecting the nation's security – capably, efficiently and with restraint.

Jonathan Pearlman

MISSION IMPOSSIBLE

Spying in the age of Xi and Zoom

Andrew Davies

As the world shifts, so do intelligence practices. An intelligence analyst at her desk today worrying about the accuracy of COVID-19
data from China, the origins of a persistent cyberattack or the machi-
nations of a terrorist group with undercover cells in half a dozen
countries probably doesn't spend a lot of time reflecting on how much
easier her job would have been thirty years ago. But recent developments in geopolitics and technology, as well as a continuing terrorism
threat, have been complicating the lives of Australia's intelligence
community. And these changes have occurred as the nation's spy
agencies have been emerging from the shadows, which carries the risk
of any misjudgements or failures being more widely exposed.

The current intelligence era began in 1991, with the collapse of
the Soviet Union – the culmination of a battle of intelligence that
had lasted forty years. During the Cold War, long careers began and

ended with the same adversary and many of the same intelligence challenges in place. In the absence of open conflict between the main protagonists – notwithstanding several proxy wars – states were determined to strengthen their intelligence capabilities, and their efforts to do so helped to reshape the international order. The United States, for instance, set up a global espionage network that leveraged its alliance relationships. The Five Eyes collaboration between the United States, Australia, Canada, New Zealand and the United Kingdom established intelligence collection sites around the world and took advantage of geography to split intelligence responsibilities between members.

Then the Berlin Wall came down and, in the wave of liberal democratic triumphalism that followed the Soviet Union's demise, academics wondered if boredom and ennui would be the greatest challenges of the twenty-first century. In the 1990s, as security issues took a back seat to economics and trade liberalisation, the budgets of intelligence agencies came under strong downward pressure. As well, America's allies, including Australia, found themselves less central to Washington's strategic thinking than they had been for decades. The intelligence-sharing relationship continued, but without the cachet it had during the Cold War. For Australia's intelligence community, boredom was bad for business.

Of course, history didn't come to an end in 1991. After a brief interlude of relative calm in which the West congratulated itself for a job well done and globalised its economy, the bipolar Cold War gave way to a more diverse geopolitical landscape that generated a range of less predictable threats. The September 11 attacks changed the focus of intelligence agencies drastically. But other, less dramatic changes also had profound consequences. The globalisation of economic activity enabled the rise of China as a major economic and geopolitical player, and hopes that the People's Republic of China would want to play by the established rules were sadly dashed. Technology also made the world a smaller and more connected place. The internet brought huge benefits, but it also allowed criminals, terrorists and state-backed hackers to reach into governments, economies and polities around the world.

If those challenges weren't enough, today intelligence agencies find themselves competing in an information marketplace with a diverse array of news and opinion sources – many of which are reporting in real time and on a 24/7 news cycle – for the attention of their government and military customers. While some world leaders continue to place a premium on the covert collection methods and analytic expertise of the intelligence community, others emphatically do not. The CIA learnt that the hard way in early 2019 when the organisation's chief, Gina Haspel, contradicted what Donald Trump had decided about Iran's weapon programs and was told – via Twitter – that "Intelligence should go back to school". In January 2020, it seems that warnings from the intelligence community about the impending COVID-19 pandemic resulted in few immediate policy responses anywhere in the West. Intelligence is always just one of many factors that governments weigh up, and sometimes it is not the most important.

It doesn't help that the most public intelligence work of the past few decades concerned making a case for Iraq's continued pursuit of weapons of mass destruction in the prelude to the 2003 war. Although that war and the disastrous occupation that followed was as much a policy failure as an intelligence one, intelligence organisations were significantly damaged by being seen to have accommodated the wishes of their political masters.

It is difficult to rebuild the public's trust when intelligence successes tend to remain in the shadows while failures become all too public. And with the wealth of information resources (of variable quality) now available to anyone with an internet connection, the government can no longer merely invoke secret intelligence to justify its actions and expect a sceptical public to accept it.

Intelligence about the impending pandemic resulted in few immediate policy responses

A homegrown intelligence community

At the height of the Cold War, Australia's intelligence community had no public visibility. But a growing scepticism caused by the failure to find weapons of mass destruction after the Iraq War, an increase in the budgets and powers of the intelligence agencies as they began to focus on terrorism, and the onset of the digital age have made the public much more likely to question the government's motives for its security policies. In recent years, the Australian Security Intelligence Organisation (ASIO) and the national signals intelligence agency, the Australian Signals Directorate, have responded by disclosing some of their operational approaches and challenges in public addresses and online, including on social media. Old-school spies would have recoiled. But the agencies are less likely to establish trust and credibility if they maintain an impenetrable veil of secrecy.

The current shape of Australia's national intelligence community dates back to December 2018, when it was expanded and reorganised after a major review commissioned by the Turnbull government. But it has been a work-in-progress for more than seventy years; today's agencies originated in World War II, though they took on their current form in the early years of the Cold War. In fact, ASIO came into being partly at the behest of Australia's allies, who were concerned that we offered a soft way into the West for Soviet intelligence.

The regulation in the first few decades of Australian intelligence was much lighter than today. The agencies were not publicly acknowledged before the 1970s, and they worked under ministerial direction with no significant independent oversight. Perhaps not surprisingly, at times there was some cavalier behaviour. The Whitlam government had serious doubts about the political neutrality of its intelligence agencies, especially ASIO. Attorney-General Lionel Murphy went so far as to make a midnight journey to the ASIO offices to search for material the government suspected was being withheld.

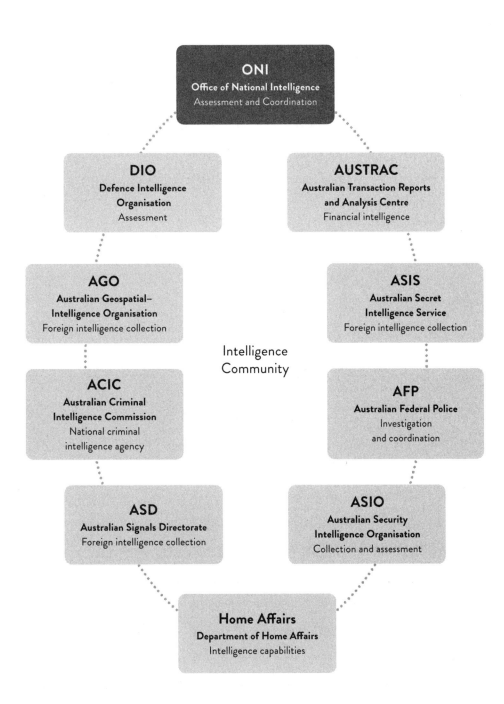

ONI
Office of National Intelligence
Assessment and Coordination

DIO
Defence Intelligence
Organisation
Assessment

AUSTRAC
Australian Transaction Reports
and Analysis Centre
Financial intelligence

AGO
Australian Geospatial–
Intelligence Organisation
Foreign intelligence collection

ASIS
Australian Secret
Intelligence Service
Foreign intelligence collection

Intelligence
Community

ACIC
Australian Criminal
Intelligence Commission
National criminal
intelligence agency

AFP
Australian Federal Police
Investigation
and coordination

ASD
Australian Signals Directorate
Foreign intelligence collection

ASIO
Australian Security
Intelligence Organisation
Collection and assessment

Home Affairs
Department of Home Affairs
Intelligence capabilities

The current shape of Australia's intelligence community dates back to December 2018, but it has been a work-in-progress for more than seventy years.

In 1974, Whitlam convened a royal commission under Justice Robert Hope with the aim of reforming the intelligence community. Its findings led to legislation responsible for much of the structure in place today, such as ASIO's codified roles and apolitical character. Interestingly, the commission found that the Australian intelligence community was too close to its Five Eyes partners and not sufficiently responsive to Australian institutions – an observation perhaps prompted by the commission being denied access to the joint US–Australian facility at Pine Gap.

But cultural change took time – and another royal commission under Justice Hope. Announced in 1983 by prime minister Bob Hawke after the Combe–Ivanov scandal – which involved a former national secretary of the Labor Party along with a Soviet agent working out of the embassy in Canberra – the second royal commission established the building blocks of today's intelligence community.

The need for this second inquiry was exemplified in late 1983, as the commission was underway. In a bungled Australian Secret Intelligence Service training exercise in Melbourne's Sheraton Hotel, a member of the public was manhandled and others threatened by operatives wearing masks and carrying pistols. The incident was later described by Hope as "poorly planned, poorly prepared and poorly co-ordinated".

The findings resulted in the establishment of an independent statutory office, the Inspector-General of Intelligence and Security (IGIS) – in many ways a standing royal commissioner – and the establishment of a multi-party parliamentary joint committee. The final major reform occurred when the foreign intelligence–collection agencies were brought under legislation with the passing of the *Intelligence Services Act 2001*. Australian intelligence was then under ministerial, statutory, legislative and parliamentary oversight, and the excesses of previous times became almost unthinkable. That was perhaps just as well, as the Act was passed only a few weeks after the September 11 attacks, which ushered in a whole new intelligence focus – and increased tensions between intelligence work and the rights of the domestic population.

The September 11 shake-up

During the Cold War, most Western intelligence and security organisations had a counter-terrorism branch, but such work

The powers required to operate against threats sometimes sit uncomfortably with civil liberties

was usually secondary to state-on-state espionage. That changed after the attacks that occurred on 11 September 2001, when terrorism became a major focus of the Five Eyes network. A 2013 US intelligence budget leaked by Edward Snowden showed that "combatting violent extremism" consumed fully 33 per cent of the budget, not far behind the largest budget category, "providing strategic intelligence and warning", at 39 per cent. That ratio would have been unthinkable prior to September 11.

The September 11 attacks are often described as an intelligence failure, but that is only partly true. After a series of assaults against

Western interests in Africa and the Middle East, the nature of al-Qaeda and its intent to strike Western targets, including in the United States, was well appreciated. But intelligence wasn't able to identify the individuals involved, the timing or the place of the attacks. Granular tactical information is much harder to obtain than the big-picture view, and the intelligence agencies before September 11 weren't sufficiently equipped to do that sort of analytic work.

Terrorism is, for many reasons, a much more challenging area for intelligence-gathering than state-on-state espionage. Unlike the Soviet Union government and military, which agencies had decades to get a handle on, terrorist groups don't have phone directories, rank structures and well-established communications networks. Instead of all speaking Russian or a handful of other widely spoken languages, their members speak a range of less-familiar languages and originate from diverse cultural groups, which makes it difficult for agencies to recruit suitably cleared people. Terrorist groups often form in places with weak governments, where local authorities have a limited capacity to track or circumvent their movements. Only when they aspire to the level of statehood – like the Islamic State in Syria and Iraq – do they become large-enough targets for traditional intelligence and military approaches to be effective.

When operating in the West, terrorists hide within civilian populations and make use of the same civil telecommunication infrastructure as locals. Porous borders in Europe make smuggling weapons and explosives relatively easy, and – as September 11 and

multiple attacks involving trucks driven into crowds have shown –
even everyday civilian infrastructure can be turned to use. The
close-knit and violent nature of terrorist groups makes it hard for
intelligence agencies to recruit inside sources and harder still to place
an informant.

Today's terrorist also benefits from the high-level security built
into widely available devices and apps. Finding a terrorist cell in a
city of millions of people often requires access to the common pool
of communications and the tools to sort legitimate targets from
innocent users. Potential "lone wolf" attackers, whether inspired
by extreme religious views or right-wing ideas of racial and cultural
superiority, are even harder to identify, due to a lack of links with a
parent organisation.

The powers required to operate against such threats sometimes
sit uncomfortably with civil liberties, and demand a significant level
of trust between the intelligence community and the wider Australian
polity. Despite the tremors in public confidence that followed the Iraq
weapons of mass destruction fiasco, successive Australian governments have managed to sell increased intelligence powers without
too much pushback. This has been helped by the lack of major terror
attacks in Australia, in contrast to many other Western states, due
in no small part to good intelligence work. Governments are happy
to benefit from the positive publicity of arrests and prosecutions
of would-be terrorists, which helps predispose the public to accept
the increased intrusiveness empowered by new national security

legislation for domestic security, notwithstanding scepticism on geopolitical issues. But that goodwill is not necessarily permanent. The safer the population feels, the tougher the argument for stronger laws becomes.

That is not to say that resistance to extending intelligence powers is a bad thing. There are incentives to implement stronger powers than necessary, because no government wants to be blamed for a terrorist attack on its watch. And it tends to be a one-way process: a new government doesn't want to open itself to criticism for having weakened security measures – even those that haven't proved effective – in the event of an attack. So there is effectively a ratchet on national security policy – every move tends to be towards more rather than fewer powers. Australia has enacted an extensive suite of anti-terror laws since 2001, possibly more than any comparable Western democracy. As an additional oversight mechanism, in 2011 the Gillard government created another statutory body, the Independent National Security Legislation Monitor, to review the operation, effectiveness and implications of national security and counterterrorism laws. In a democratic country, such oversight is vital to prevent excesses and to assure the community that the state's intelligence and security powers are used appropriately. Suspicions of impropriety can cause significant political ructions – as the events in the 1970s and 1980s that preceded the two royal commissions showed.

There are claims of improper behaviour by the Australian intelligence sector after those commissions, too. They include allegations that the government's signals intelligence organisation spied on unions during the 2001 Tampa affair to help the government formulate a response. Former army officer Andrew Wilkie made widely reported claims about the politicisation of Iraqi weapons of mass destruction intelligence in 2002 and 2003. The ongoing Witness K case revolves around the controversy surrounding Australian espionage against Timor-Leste during 2004 treaty negotiations. Perhaps not coincidentally, those events all took place in the early years of the *Intelligence Services Act 2001* and the IGIS's oversight. Since then, the oversight mechanism seems to have been effective, and has helped produce a culture within the intelligence community that makes breaches rare.

Australia has enacted an extensive suite of anti-terror laws since 2001

The Howard government opted not to use the substantial powers of the IGIS and commissioned its own review of the Iraqi weapons of mass destruction intelligence in 2004. The review, conducted by Philip Flood – a former head of Australia's peak intelligence agency, the Office of National Assessments – concluded (not entirely convincingly) that the intelligence had not been tailored improperly to suit the government's preferences. It is illuminating that arms-length IGIS investigations, such as the review of the Tampa affair, largely laid concerns about espionage activities to rest in the public consciousness. In contrast, the legacy of the Howard (and Bush and Blair) government continues to be dogged by perceptions of manipulation of intelligence for political ends.

In the United States, the intelligence community suffered a substantial loss of trust when the Snowden leaks and follow-up work from the press revealed that widespread interception of the public's telephony data was carried out by the National Security Agency (NSA) without valid warrants. Even worse, it seems that the oversight mechanisms had broken down. The Snowden leaks also included a description of the system used by the NSA's British equivalent that went well beyond metadata and was indiscriminate in its targeting.

Those sorts of revelations make it harder for governments to argue for greater powers, as the Abbott government found in 2014 when it tried to make the case for metadata collection in Australia (though it didn't help itself by hopelessly muddling the technical details). And the challenge is exacerbated by the public's fondness for new communications technologies that place sophisticated security mechanisms in the hands of everyday consumers.

Data mining and state secrets

Life was once much easier for Australian security agencies wanting to intercept telecommunications. When Australia's *Telecommunications (Interception and Access) Act 1979* was passed, pretty much all communications were by copper-wire telephony or telegraphy. The Act gave ASIO and the police access to communications when a warrant was obtained. Telecommunications providers – and there were far fewer of those in 1979 – had to comply as a condition of operating in Australia. With the exception of diplomatic communications to and from foreign embassies, all of the accessed communications would be unencrypted and easily exploitable for intelligence and law-enforcement purposes. Most devices were analogue, and there was no internet data to worry about.

Now, the proliferation of devices, operating systems and apps, all with proprietary protocols and security features, means that the access carriers provide under the Act is often only one element in a much longer chain. In particular, end-to-end encryption, as used by applications such as WhatsApp, Signal, iMessage and Facebook Messenger, can present huge technical hurdles. In those systems, only the two client users have the key to decrypt any message. Companies such as Apple and Facebook, on whose products the messages are transmitted, don't have access to unencrypted messages or to encryption keys.

Even the simple act of unlocking a handset can prove beyond reach, as was shown in the United States when an iPhone used by a gunman in a mass shooting became the centre of a 2016 court case. The FBI obtained a court order authorising access to the handset, but that couldn't sway Apple to comply. Apple argued that it would have to create an access channel that could be used against any iPhone on that system (though it did hand over the relevant data it could access without unlocking the phone).

Opinions were divided about Apple's position, but there was significant public support, both in the United States and here, for the privacy argument. Perhaps that reflected an increased suspicion of intelligence and security agencies following the Snowden releases. Or perhaps the public had never really appreciated the access that authorities had to analogue communications. Being able to access handsets, or read encrypted app data and communications, was not so much an additional power for the authorities as the reinstatement of long-held powers that had been diminished by technological change.

In a speech earlier this year, the head of ASIO, Mike Burgess, noted that 95 per cent of its terrorism-related investigations encountered encrypted communications. In 2018, the Turnbull government introduced legislation to require companies to assist law enforcement or intelligence with decrypting communications. The *Telecommunications and Other Legislation Amendment (Assistance and Access) Act 2018* provided new "computer access warrants", as well as search and seizure powers for computers and mobile devices to access data.

The trouble is, it's not clear that vendors of hardware and software in the global marketplace will be responsive to Australian legislative requirements. The wholesale and retail suppliers of bandwidth in Australia can be pulled into line as a condition of operating here, so the government will have access to data moving around. But the form of that data can be manipulated by apps and programs, and the devices it originates from and terminates in are manufactured with a global market in mind. High-profile companies such as Apple, Google and Facebook work with authorities when there is a clear public duty to do so, such as in identifying and eliminating child pornography.

But smaller firms from other countries might not feel such a moral obligation, especially if difficulty of access is one of their selling points. Even if an Australian government tried to make it illegal to purchase certain software, the use of virtual private networks (VPNs) and other means of avoiding geographic restrictions would make it extremely hard to enforce. The result is that while with legislative changes Australian security and intelligence agencies have clawed back some of the ground they lost in the past decade, it is unlikely they will ever again have the levels of access they enjoyed in the past.

But technology is not all a downside for the intelligence world. As well as providing the capability to collect, store and (albeit with significant limita-

Technology has opened up whole new avenues of espionage

tions) sort through vast quantities of data, it has opened up whole new avenues of espionage. The exponential growth in computing power and bandwidth over the past fifty years has revolutionised the intelligence world. Things are possible now that spies would only have dreamt of in the past, such as the collection and data mining of large quantities of telephony or messaging metadata.

The field of espionage has always been fast to adopt new technology. The 1960s saw the development of satellites that could take images of facilities and military bases deep within other nations' territories. This was followed by space-based systems that could watch for the signatures of nuclear weapons tests or the plumes from rocket launches, or collect bulk signals intelligence. The need to move that data around the globe after it was relayed to ground stations led to the creation of a network codenamed ECHELON, with ground stations in each of the Five Eyes countries and elsewhere, that has been central to Australian intelligence for decades. The new technologies didn't replace the old methods of spycraft, such as recruiting human agents, but they opened up new means of intelligence collection and data exploitation.

Probably the most significant technological development is global computer networks. When communications were predominantly through voice, interception required catching data as it passed along cables or through the air at the speed of light. But with the advent of internet communications, in many cases it became possible to target data at rest in a computer or smartphone at either end of the communications channel. Text messages, Facebook Messenger missives, emails and recordings of Zoom sessions stored on a target's devices can be downloaded and examined at leisure.

In fact, many "dirty tricks" of the past have transitioned to digital. As well as espionage, subversion and sabotage are possible over a remote computer connection. This was highlighted by the (probably) American and Israeli agencies that wrote a code designed to assume command of industrial controllers in an Iranian nuclear facility, causing the high-speed centrifuges used in uranium enrichment to exceed their operating speeds and literally tear themselves to pieces.

This type of incident also shows the enduring value of old-school espionage: a computer system that is not connected to the internet can't be hacked remotely, but if a human with access to the facility could be persuaded, the malicious code could still be uploaded directly.

The 2016 US presidential election is a well-documented case of online subversion. The cleverly orchestrated Russian social media campaign, augmented by people on the ground in the United States and the hacking of Democratic Party servers, probably made the difference between winning and losing for the Trump campaign. The ability to target individuals and key audiences through data generated by their internet use will only increase as data-mining systems become more powerful. This, combined with surveillance methods that can identify individuals among a crowd and track their movements in detail, makes for a promising future for authoritarian states looking to destabilise democratic rivals or keep an eye on their citizens.

The new, new world order

After the demise of the Soviet Union, the United States saw itself as the hub of a "new world order", which would see the triumph of globalised free trade and a wave of democratisation. It didn't work out that way. Nation-building attempts in Afghanistan and Iraq failed, and states such as North Korea and Iran continued to go their own way. But the most drastic challenge to the established order has come from China. Geopolitical optimists expected the PRC to make itself comfortable within existing structures – what Australia's 2016 Defence White Paper deemed "the rules-based international order" – and to slowly liberalise its economy and polity over time. But, as its strength has increased, it has become clear that China has its own preferred set of rules. And that is as true in espionage as it is in geopolitics.

The organisation and practices of a nation's intelligence agencies tend to reflect both the character of the underlying polity and the country's strengths and weaknesses. The Soviet-era KGB excelled at infiltrating sensitive positions in the West, including here in Australia, where it managed to recruit public servants and ministerial staff to provide information on Australia and its allies. The Soviets had an agent within the wire fence during the Manhattan Project, and others in many Western counterintelligence agencies – including ASIO. Those high-level "human intelligence" skills were honed through the KGB's domestic role in supporting the continued single-party rule of the Communist Party. Alongside its international remit, the KGB was tasked with keeping an eye on incipient subversion within the Soviet bloc, and ethnic minority and religious groups were routinely penetrated by KGB informers. Meanwhile, on the other side of the Iron Curtain, the CIA had no domestic security role and operated in a political system whose legitimacy was not under serious threat. Generous budgets allowed it to harness the technical innovation and industrialisation that propelled the United States to global-power status in the twentieth century. While the CIA and its alliance partners ran human agents, Western espionage had technology at its core.

The elaborate developments included extensive space-based systems and specialised nuclear submarines for tapping seabed cables.

We should expect China to pursue its interests by making use of its natural advantages – not least its vast reserves of human power, which allows for the collection and sifting of very large quantities of information, and the reach and influence of the Chinese diaspora. And the norms of espionage that have long been accepted in the West won't necessarily apply, as was seen when the Obama administration took issue with Chinese industrial espionage. The United States accepts state-on-state espionage for national security purposes – after all, that was the raison d'être of the Cold War – but regards purely commercial interests as out of bounds. Yet for the Chinese Communist Party – which owns many of China's industries, in any case – economic growth and prosperity is an intrinsic part of its legitimacy and so indivisible from national security.

The norms of espionage that have long been accepted in the West won't necessarily apply

British archaeologist and historian Ian Morris commented at an Australian Strategic Policy Institute conference in 2011 that he wasn't sure liberal democracy would survive the twenty-first century. That is a gloomy prognostication, but trends in technology and the success of subversive activities in recent years mean that it can't be easily dismissed. It remains to be seen which states will suffer or benefit most from COVID-19, for example, but China quickly tried to take advantage of the crisis for geopolitical gain. The increasing assertiveness of Chinese and Russian intelligence comes – not coincidentally – as liberal democracies are struggling with internal divisions that undermine confidence in their state institutions, including their intelligence agencies.

The future of spying

Intelligence agencies tend to become comfortable with one model of the world and can develop a mindset that blinds them to indicators of changes ahead. Failures occur, sometimes around the biggest issues. For example, while there were plenty of signs for an alert analyst to see that the economy and political structures of the Soviet Union were shaky, its rapid disintegration in 1990–91 surprised many in the intelligence world. After forty years of intensive Cold War espionage, a world without the Soviets was unimaginable. As long-time CIA analyst Jack Davis observed, "The advantage of mind-sets is that they help analysts get the production out on time and keep things going effectively between those watershed events that become chapter headings in the history books."

For the intelligence community, continuity is much easier to foresee than dislocation, and there is a constant demand for reports and briefings about today's world. The challenge is to keep up with routine but important work while still providing strategic warning of future events.

Twenty years ago, it would have been hard to predict that attention would shift from traditional state-on-state espionage to international terrorism, or that cyberspace would soon allow foreign actors to seriously interfere with elections in advanced democracies. Twenty years from now, the practice and subjects of intelligence work will have changed again. China's growth and its clear intentions to stamp its preferences on the international order will require an increased focus on intelligence-gathering and a swing back towards state-on-state espionage. Protecting Western intellectual property and military secrets will be a continuing counterintelligence challenge. And, given China's increased assertiveness in the South and East China seas, its open loathing of Japan, and the Chinese Communist Party's stated ambition of reuniting Taiwan before the 2049 centenary of its rise to power, Chinese military capabilities and leadership intentions will be of enduring interest to Western intelligence organisations.

Machine learning and decision-making systems have the potential to transform any analytic work based on data inputs, as well as making it possible to manipulate people and systems in new and subtle ways – the influence operations run by Cambridge Analytica and Russian intelligence in recent years only hint at the possibilities.

By 2040, the impacts of climate change will be impossible to avoid. And the geopolitical landscape will have again shifted, possibly in surprising directions. The way those factors, and others we are yet to appreciate, interact will require deep expertise to navigate, including language skills and a sophisticated cultural understanding of rival states.

One silver lining from the COVID-19 crisis is that the value of fact-based analysis and expert advice has been demonstrated. The dreadful outcomes in the United States and many Western European countries indicate what can go wrong when expertise is not at the centre of decision-making. And history is full of examples of inadequate or incomplete intelligence work leading to strategic shocks and tactical failures, such as September 11 and Pearl Harbor. The challenge now facing Australia's agents and analysts is not just to grapple with diverse threats and increasingly complex technology, but also to ensure that their reports are deemed credible and given due weight in policy deliberations – even when they are offering information and advice that decision-makers or the public may not want to hear. ■

DATA DRIVEN

How COVID-19
and cyberspace are
changing spycraft

Danielle Cave

In mid-November 2019, WeChat users in China started discussing a new virus spreading in Wuhan. The words and phrases *SARS*, *coronavirus*, *novel coronavirus*, *Feidian* (the Chinese equivalent of SARS), *shortness of breath*, *dyspnea* and *diarrhoea* all began to increase in use across China's most popular messaging app. As the virus spread, volunteer open-source researchers in China began collecting and archiving online material, including through GitHub, a Microsoft-owned coding and collaboration platform, to protect and preserve information at risk from China's internet censors. Later, some of these open-source researchers, web archivists and citizen journalists would be detained, their online projects shuttered.

We will never know how many governments were monitoring and collecting these early signs of COVID-19, and we will only hear snippets about what they found. Like advice from public health agencies and diplomatic cables, intelligence provides another source of information for governments. And for those intelligence agencies that pivoted quickly as the virus spread around the world in early 2020, online open-source collection, including data scraped from Chinese social media networks, blogs and archived databases, had the potential to alert them to the seriousness of what was to come.

On 6 January 2020, eight days before the now infamous tweet by the World Health Organization announcing that Chinese authorities had "found no clear evidence of human-to-human transmission of the novel #coronavirus", cyberespionage actor APT32 was on the hunt, trying to find out more about the unnamed virus spreading in Wuhan and beyond. APT32 (also known as OceanLotus), long believed by cyber-security researchers to be operating on behalf of the Vietnamese government, used COVID-19-themed malicious email attachments in an attempt to compromise the professional and personal email accounts of officials working for the government of Wuhan and China's Ministry of Emergency Management.

We don't know how successful APT32's attempted cyber intrusions were, or what prompted this operation. But we do know that Vietnam – like Australia – acted quickly, closing its 1400-kilometre border with China on 1 February. By the end of April, the Vietnamese government had reported no deaths and fewer than 300 cases of COVID-19.

Alongside most industries, intelligence agencies – including

Australia's – will be assessing whether the global disruption caused by COVID-19 will change the way they operate. Will it accelerate evolutions in tradecraft? Will the expectations and priorities of intelligence customers shift as these types of global events become more frequent?

They will need to take stock of their response. As the virus began its rampant spread, were they set up and resourced to respond in a timely fashion? Crucially, as other sources of information signalled danger, were they able to move fast to collect information, much of which, in the early stages at least, was not necessarily "secret"? For governments wrestling with difficult decisions such as border closures and public safety measures, having accurate data about the virus and its spread was essential.

> **In China, collecting on-the-ground human intelligence is becoming more dangerous and expensive**

But responding quickly isn't always easy because intelligence collection is challenging, labour-intensive and complicated. Agencies can't ordinarily pivot quickly between targets. In China, which has invested heavily in sophisticated surveillance and public security technologies to monitor and control its population, collecting on-the-ground human intelligence is becoming more dangerous and expensive. The demands of dealing with, and protecting, sources means that human intelligence may not be easily redirected. Signals intelligence also needs time to change course; penetrating a network requires figuring out a way in, and exploitable vulnerabilities are hard to find. Only certain intelligence collectors, like those working in open source and geospatial information gathering, can manoeuvre more readily.

Intelligence collection during the early months of COVID-19 would have required agencies to work creatively and flexibly. They would have had to gather information, much of which only existed in, for example, municipal and provincial medical circles, high-resolution satellite imagery or archived online databases and Chinese social media channels. This would have raised another challenge for intelligence agencies: as the data poured in, were they able to quickly process and analyse what they had?

But the most important questions are the ones that can't be answered yet. With nations still emerging from this crisis, intelligence communities need to forecast what a world after COVID-19 abates will look like. Because they need to make decisions now about how they will operate in this new environment.

Spying in cyberspace

For as long as – and perhaps even longer than – than there have been states, there have been spies. In Australia, the intelligence community comprises not just those in the field but also those conducting analytical, technical, signals, operational and geospatial functions.

Today, all of this work is being transformed by exponential changes in cyberspace and technology. Relatively cheap, everyday devices can be far more valuable sources of intelligence than a wire-tap or a bug installed in a light fitting. A fridge that alerts someone when they need butter, cheese or ice-cream, and relays that information over the internet to them and their grocery store, provides not just an insight into their diet and the condition of their arteries, but also the potential capability to listen, watch and learn about that person, all from a safe distance. Apps on a smartphone are opportunities to learn about a person's habits, to listen in on their conversations, to steal their data and to understand what makes them tick – and what may make them vulnerable. Researchers in the United States, Japan and China have demonstrated they can secretly activate artificial intelligence–powered virtual assistants (such as Siri) by shining laser pointers at their microphones and sending them commands undetectable to the human ear. Few people completely separate their work and home lives, and in a work-from-home environment it's almost impossible, making the exploitation of these devices more valuable for intelligence agencies.

However, much online collection relies on more overt, but often hard to find, sources. The ability to hoover up multi-language social media content (and its associated metadata), foreign government documents, databases and traditional foreign media reporting is becoming increasingly important as more of the world's population and activities move online. This open-source collection is cheap, quick and can provide in-depth understanding of countries where traditional diplomatic reporting is hampered by a lack of official access and where it may be too difficult to operate a sustainable pipeline of on-the-ground collection.

For domestic security agencies such as ASIO, and other parts of the Australian government involved in counterespionage and foreign interference, the fact that almost everyone leaves a trace online makes the internet a powerful tool to investigate companies and individuals that are not entirely who they say they are. Including those, for example, who may be covertly operating as "cutouts" (intermediaries) for a foreign state, posing a threat to Australia's national security.

Conversely, cyberspace provides more avenues for counter-intelligence adversaries to identify our spies. Social media companies are equipped with algorithms that, based on possible social, work and education ties, connect potential "friends", and these algorithms operate surprisingly well in the absence of any publicly acknowledged connections. Over the last five years, some of these companies have integrated facial recognition technologies into their platforms, making it easier – for both the platform and adversaries – to analyse photos and videos. Such features, which tend to be opt-in by default, also work on historical data (including old photos, which could geo-locate rookie spies in unusual places – for example, one town over from an isolated joint defence–intelligence training facility).

All of this is hazardous territory for modern spies, especially those working undercover. They may have to be online for work reasons, and may want to be for social reasons. And if they're not online, that only raises suspicions among those around them and those they meet for work purposes.

Some countries are also investing in increasingly sophisticated smart cities that connect public security technologies such as facial, gait and licence recognition with traffic, airport and hotel databases. These systems can be multi-use – a system to monitor and manage traffic flow might also be finetuned to help unearth fly-in fly-out intelligence operations. The CIA reportedly stopped conducting certain types of operations in Singapore in the early 2000s because of a security services database that incorporated real-time flight, border control, hotel and taxi data. As national security reporters Jenna McLaughlin and Zach Dorfman observed, "If it took too long for a traveler to get from the airport to a hotel in a taxi, the anomaly would trigger an alert."

The internet is not just changing the work of collectors, but of analysts

The internet is not just changing the work of collectors, but of analysts. These analysts make sense of global trends for politicians, senior public servants and military officials, and often become the face of an issue or geographic region. But their reporting is no longer derived exclusively from classified material; today, an analyst spends significant time switching between their "high side" (classified/secret) and their "low side" computers (those we all have).

One reason for this is, while they may write for a small group of influential "customers" – in the case of Australia's Office of National Intelligence, for example, the key customer is the prime minister – the terms of that monogamous relationship aren't reciprocated. In 2020, these customers have information at their fingertips – online news, think-tank blogs, Twitter, messaging apps. They are more informed than ever about the topics they work on, but also more distracted, and at risk of getting stuck in echo chambers. Analysts now have to know what information their key customers are consuming, and how they consume it, so they can pitch their reports accordingly.

As cosy as it may be for analysts to live only in the air-gapped world of secret intelligence, it is now essential to combine both worlds – the classified and unclassified. The onset of COVID-19 demonstrated this challenge: how to quickly make sense of the different streams of intelligence and other reporting flowing in through open-source and classified channels about the spread of a new, unnamed virus?

COVID-19 and intelligence collection

Due to the opacity of China's party-state system and the tight control of its media, online and physical environments, the advent of COVID-19 was accompanied by an information void that the world's governments – including their intelligence agencies – had to try to fill. It soon became clear that the Chinese state was suppressing and censoring information about the initial outbreak, as well as the ongoing extent of infection and death rates. For the world's decisions-makers, who were trying to make sense of these events and their international implications, diplomatic reporting and new online intelligence-collection techniques – particularly open source – provided crucial glimpses into the crisis.

As the first reports of a new illness in Wuhan emerged in December 2019, the potential targets for intelligence agencies were fairly obvious – institutions in China that held key medical and public security data. This included hospitals in badly affected areas, certain ministries (such as Health, Public Security, Defence, Science and Technology) and officials in key local and national positions.

Thanks to comments from US officials, and Chinese and Taiwanese media reports, we know that Chinese social media also offered a rich vein of open-source intelligence collection, particularly from November 2019 to January 2020, before China's internet censors sprung into action.

The Wuhan Municipal Health Commission did not release its first public notice on the disease until 31 December 2019 (incidentally, this notice was then archived online by netizens more than 400 times between 6 January and 18 May). But prior to this, hints were already online, awaiting discovery. For example, analysis of WeChat data between 17 November and 30 December 2019 by researchers at Xi'an Jiaotong University's Department of Infectious Diseases found that the use of certain keywords such as *coronavirus* increased.

The last day of 2019 marked an increase in online censorship in China. For intelligence agencies, the removal and absence of information is telling, highlighting topics that authorities are working to hide from public view. During a crisis, such censorship (which, in the case of WeChat and Weibo, is tracked by academics in Hong Kong) can provide a trail to follow.

Taiwan, which has had a very successful response to COVID-19, can partly attribute this to the close online connections between its netizens and China's. One of the reasons the government acted so quickly was reportedly because early notices published by the Wuhan Municipal Health Commission were reposted to PTT – a popular student-led discussion forum in Taiwan with more than 1.5 million registered users. The reposted notices apparently came to the attention of senior Taiwanese health officials.

But foreign governments were also likely interested in developments far beyond China and probably had plenty of questions for their diplomats and intelligence officials. How were other major economic and security partners coping with the crisis? Had their militaries been affected? How had the world's top medical institutions been advancing on developing a vaccine?

The FBI revealed in April 2020 that foreign states were engaged in cyberespionage against US medical research institutions, such as hospitals and labs, studying the novel coronavirus. Around the same time, cybersecurity companies across the world began warning their clients to prepare for increased targeting, particularly of the governmental, healthcare and biotech sectors. China too has complained about hacking attempts. Back in February, China's largest cyber-security company, Qihoo 360, claimed a South Asian–based APT group was behind cyberattacks targeting China's medical sector.

Another target, of course, has been the World Health Organization (WHO). The United Nations' lead agency on global health issues has struggled to disentangle itself from the politics surrounding COVID-19 – not hugely surprising given the state of US–China relations and the nature of multilateral agencies (they can be as political as the nations jostling for influence inside and around them). The WHO's overreliance on data from an authoritarian state with a proven record of information manipulation and censorship made it a prime intelligence target. Its leadership dynamics and decision-making processes, the

Some states working on COVID-19 have very likely included the WHO in their intelligence collection

influence of its member states and the contents of internal classified reporting all likely became of interest. The public only ever receives fleeting insights into what is consuming the world's espionage actors, but we know that some states working on COVID-19 have very likely included the WHO in their intelligence collection. Cyberespionage operatives linked to Vietnam, Iran and South Korea, for example, have reportedly been among the APT groups targeting the work and personal email accounts of WHO staff, including by creating a string of malicious messages and websites designed to trick recipients into inputting information by mimicking Google services.

Defending its handling of the outbreak, the United States government has been unusually open about its COVID-19 intelligence collection in China. On 9 April, US Air Force general John Hyten, vice-chairman of the Joint Chiefs of Staff, told journalists he did not see intelligence reports on the coronavirus until January: "We went back and looked at everything in November and December. The first indication we have were the reports out of China in late December that were in the public forum. And the first intel reports I saw were in January." Similar candour on the topics and timeline of information collection, so close to the fact, would be extraordinary coming from the media-shy Australian intelligence community. But in the United States, exactly what the administration did and didn't know in the early weeks of the outbreak became a matter of intense public interest due to the country's struggle to contain the virus.

On 27 April, *The Washington Post* reported that US intelligence agencies issued warnings about the coronavirus in more than a dozen classified briefings prepared for President Trump in January and February. This highlights the Achilles heel of intelligence communities the world over. Just because a report is written, and even read by senior figures in government, does not mean it influences the government's actions or policies. Intelligence can be politicised, misunderstood or ignored. In the digital age, decision-makers are bombarded by information – it's up to intelligence chiefs, and their deputies, to ensure that urgent reports get attention. As former US secretary of state and national security advisor Henry Kissinger reportedly said after an analyst reminded him that he had been warned about the impending outbreak of war, "You warned me, but you didn't convince me."

The data explosion

Humans are social animals. We're suckers for tools that help us engage with the world. Cyberspace is a domain of 4.5 billion internet users. This yearning to connect will usher in billions more internet users and tens of billions of additional smart devices over the coming years.

The typical internet user jumps between multiple online networks without much thought, depending on where they live, how old they are, where they work, the languages they speak and who they are talking to. Facebook, Twitter, WhatsApp, Instagram, Google, LINE, WeChat, TikTok, Signal, Slack, Spotify, Skype, Zoom, Weibo ... we hop between them on our low-end or high-end smartphones. Because of COVID-19, we've widened the digital buffet to include more teleconferencing, health and lifestyle apps.

All these activities – and the proliferation of connected technologies across industry and in our homes – provide new access points for gathering intelligence. But they also generate data, mountains and mountains of it. And this issue – the proliferation of data in an interconnected world – is reshaping modern spycraft.

As my now-colleague Nathan Ruser discovered, data from even the most innocuous mobile applications, such as a fitness-tracking app, can be harnessed in creative ways to unearth sensitive information. When Strava launched their "heatmap", which aggregated data from 13 trillion GPS points and one billion activities, they failed to foresee that geo-coding years of Strava fitness activity would reveal patterns and locations that some, especially governments, have spent a small fortune trying to keep secret. Ruser tripped up governments around the world by revealing this with a single tweet on 28 January 2018. The heatmap allowed the general public, and our adversaries, to sift through data that revealed undisclosed foreign military bases and intelligence facilities and appeared to show Strava activity inside secure facilities where electronic devices are supposed to be checked at the front door. The map even showed a lone cyclist pedalling around the US Air Force base known as "Area 51". It also revealed the fitness routes of military and government officials posted overseas, providing malicious actors with intelligence about where and when these people were out exercising, and were likely alone.

In all my conversations with security officials this year and last, it became clear that it wasn't the collection of data that was keeping senior figures awake at night. Rather, it was dealing with the data after it had been collected.

The challenges of this data-drenched world were highlighted in a February 2020 speech by ASIO's director-general of security, Mike Burgess (also the former director-general of the Australian Signals Directorate). Presenting his inaugural annual threat assessment, he said: "We need people who can out-think and out-imagine our adversaries, and who can harness the power of technology and data alongside good old-fashioned relationship-building."

When I followed up after his speech with questions to help inform this essay, Burgess told me: "There has been an explosion of data. Things used to be more simple ... Now, there's a huge amount of data associated with whatever you're collecting. The data-rich environment we operate in today is both a challenge and an opportunity."

In Australia – unlike some other states – collection of information occurs under strict accountability mechanisms, including stringent legislation, and oversight by the Inspector-General of Intelligence and Security and the Parliamentary Joint Committee on Intelligence and Security.

The proliferation of data in an interconnected world is reshaping modern spycraft

Agencies in Australia cannot undertake the type of wholesale domestic data collection China can, for example, such as through social media networks, the social credit system, and by using new technologies to target ethnic groups like the Uighur and Tibetan populations. But advances in collection techniques mean there is still a huge volume of international information available to collect.

Over the next decade, intelligence communities will spend much of their time trying to figure out how to host, process and use all of this data, which only holds value if it can be analysed. Have they made the right investments in their IT, digital and technological systems to cope with the explosion of data? What potential do machine-learning technologies offer in terms of big data analytics, and trend and predictive analysis? How will developments in quantum computing and artificial intelligence affect their capabilities? And how will our adversaries exploit the power and proliferation of our data?

Intelligence adversaries and state hackers

One of the largest US intelligence failures of this century involved a penetration of the CIA's covert internet-based communications system, which allowed remote messaging between the agency and its sources. The breach, which is thought to have begun in 2010 and continued until 2013, started in Iran and proliferated to other countries, including China.

A series of digital mistakes paved the way for this catastrophe, which reportedly resulted in the executions of Chinese and Iranian sources. As outlined by Jenna McLaughlin and Zach Dorfman, an interim communications system set up for new recruits was accidentally linked to the permanent system to which the CIA transitioned their vetted sources. Another problem was that a link could be made between the covert communications system and the US government.

China was allegedly so determined to compromise the system that it set up a special task force, including members of the Ministry of State Security and the military's signals directorate. It appears as though Iran and China each cracked the system independently. Around the same time as the CIA's China network was demolished,

CIA assets in Russia started to disappear. This reportedly occurred after a joint training session between Chinese and Russian intelligence officers.

According to Dorfman and McLaughlin, the Iranians unravelled the wider CIA network using search terms to identify the website that the CIA was relying on to communicate with its agents. Once they found one website, they looked for others with similar digital signifiers, "eventually hitting on the right string of advanced search terms to locate other secret CIA websites".

The compromise shows the stark dangers of underestimating sophisticated cyber actors, particularly authoritarian states that have developed their capabilities through mass surveillance of their citizens and domestic control of the internet.

States such as China, Russia and Iran are gaining an intelligence edge over the West. Minimal accountability at home means these states can go beyond espionage, engaging in intellectual property theft and foreign interference. But Western governments don't always help themselves, and can create confusion about what is acceptable behaviour, particularly in cyberspace. The widespread US intelligence-gathering, and perceived overreach, revealed by Edward Snowden's leaking of classified intelligence from 2013 entrenched distrust among some allies and partners, particularly in Europe. This has been exacerbated by President Trump's tendency to publicly berate allies while praising Russian president Vladimir Putin and dictators such as North Korea's Kim Jong-un.

Western governments, despite a commitment to democracy, have also enabled features of closed societies to flourish domestically. In Australia, we claim to have an "open, free and secure cyberspace", flying our diplomats around the world to advocate for this in multilateral forums. Yet it's no longer true. For years now, we have permitted censored and surveilled social media networks based out of China, such as WeChat, to operate locally, with minimal oversight compared with their American counterparts, like Facebook (which we regularly, and rightly, scrutinise).

China, Russia, North Korea and Iran have invested significantly in their cyberespionage capabilities – and this is paying off, including in Australia. You would fast become wealthy if you bet on the Chinese state every time the Australian government announced a "sophisticated state actor" was behind the latest cyberattack or attempted hack of parliament, or a political party, government department, university, think tank or business.

In January 2020, former deputy director-general of the Australian Signals Directorate, Simeon Gilding, who finished in the role in 2019, spoke briefly but frankly in the only media interview he has ever given: "China has form over a decade of large-scale hacks of our networks." Former prime minister Malcolm Turnbull elaborated further in his autobiography:

While many nations sought to spy on Australia, China represented by far the bulk of detected activity. It was mostly cyberespionage, generally managed by intelligence agencies in Shanghai. Their appetite for information seemed limitless, ranging from businesses to universities to government departments, and much else besides. It was on an industrial scale.

This has been well known across Canberra's security community for the better part of a decade. But it is rarely, if ever, publicly acknowledged. Persistent self-censorship has deepened the disconnect between what is known in small circles, largely in government, and what is known by everyone else.

China, Russia and Iran are gaining an intelligence edge over the West

In Australia, we have repeatedly failed to have public conversations about our complicated relationship with China. Our largest trading partner is also our largest intelligence adversary. This is inconvenient, and the consequences can, at times, be messy. It presents challenges that will continue to impact on national security and parts of the economy. It raises concerns about issues such as data privacy and academic freedom, and places groups like Chinese-language media, civil society and diaspora communities at risk from foreign interference and coercion. But the complexities of this relationship won't change anytime soon. Our political leaders need to learn how to talk about it. Failing to engage the public on major policies as they are announced – as in

August 2018, when the Australian government banned "high-risk vendors" from the 5G network, leaving the explanation to a media release – draws attention to already sensitive issues and invites speculation. Avoiding this will require talking to the public in more detail, and more often, and giving senior bureaucrats greater licence to publicly acknowledge today's realities.

Wired for the next disruption

As the world emerges from this crisis, intelligence agencies – including Australia's – will be assessing whether current operating models are fit for purpose in a changed environment.

COVID-19 has demonstrated to intelligence collectors around the world that they will be expected to redeploy against a wide range of unusual targets – from a hospital in Wuhan to the inner chambers of the WHO in Geneva to medical labs developing vaccines. In the short term, it has created new opportunities, especially for signals intelligence agencies, as the world's politicians, business leaders and government officials began working from home, hopping onto unencrypted teleconferencing tools and social apps – some with controversial credentials. But agencies will need to find ways to work effectively in a new environment that may limit their time in secure buildings and their access to secret systems. They may need to rely more on technologies that will not always compensate for a loss of face-to-face contact with human sources and colleagues. Spies can't always teleconference like the rest of us.

In the long term, the pandemic raises questions about intelligence services' abilities to respond to rapid and unexpected change. COVID-19 was a black swan event – difficult to predict, but enormously consequential. There will likely be others. Climate change, in particular, will dramatically increase the frequency and severity of natural hazards. Yet the more predictable challenges, or "white swans", such as foreign interference and cyberespionage, will remain. Traditional spycraft will need to evolve to balance these threats.

In the meantime, easier access to data and new technologies is lowering the entry costs into the murky world of espionage. Smaller intelligence outfits, like those of North Korea, Vietnam and Israel, have gained outsized influence by investing in hackers, focusing on the collection of strategic datasets, and by mastering or combining certain technologies, such as facial and gait recognition systems. Private intelligence outfits, often brimming with former Israeli and American spies, can give smaller states a leg-up – as former National Security Agency hackers did when they helped the United Arab Emirates to spy on its citizens, journalists and human rights dissidents, and even to target Americans.

The role of our intelligence agencies will continue to expand beyond collection. The Australian Signals Directorate's involvement in informing Australia's decision to ban 5G "high-risk vendors" was unique for the agency. But 5G was only the beginning. The skill sets in some of these agencies are not found in other parts of the public service. When it comes to critical and emerging technologies, this knowledge will be called upon, more and more often, to help inform major policy decisions.

Authoritarian states may be gaining an edge, but the social and political control of their own populations depends on online and surveillance technologies that can also be used against them. Likewise, all governments have made use of mobile, public security and biometric technologies to track and tackle the spread of COVID-19. Keeping some of these systems in place might have health or security benefits, but may also assist adversaries.

Counterespionage is becoming increasingly difficult as targets use encrypted communications to hide their tracks. Foreign interference is more common, and more nuanced, as some states turn to lawfare (the use or misuse of legal systems to target critics), disinformation and social media manipulation, and coercion and threats aimed at businesses, academics and others to interfere in political debate. Tracking and countering these tactics is not easy. "We have to plug every hole, they just have to find one hole," Mike Burgess told me when we talked about adversaries in the digital era.

This whack-a-mole challenge, which will only become more difficult as more parts of our lives connect to cyberspace, will require Australia's intelligence community to innovate. It will need to rethink its workforce. Does it have the right people and mix of skills? Not yet. On gender alone, many agencies still carry more gaps than their policy peers. Women are far less likely than their male counterparts to be found in senior operational, analytical or overseas roles, or leading major policy-shaping activities such as independent reviews. The community is also likely to need more big data analysts, technologists, China and counterespionage specialists, and people from diverse ethnic and cultural backgrounds. It will also need people with strategic thinking and entrepreneurial skills – to generate new ideas and lead on changes that will guarantee success in a world after COVID-19.

As billions more netizens and smart devices come online around the world, conquering data will be essential. Collecting data is the easier part; analysing it is hard, and storing huge datasets can be astronomically expensive. Finding the needles in the haystack will require financial investment, a greater use of emerging technologies such as machine learning and the right mixture of analysts.

Our intelligence chiefs will increasingly have to come out of the shadows to talk to the public

Our intelligence chiefs will increasingly have to come out of the shadows to talk to and engage with the public. Major decisions, emerging threats and increases in public spending, particularly when cyber and technology issues are involved, need to be explained, and justified, by the government.

COVID-19 and its effects will continue to be disruptive, but this pandemic is also a unique chance for the Australian intelligence community to prepare for the future and test current assumptions about what our world could look like. Agencies will need to balance long-term priorities with the urgent and unexpected: they must continue to focus on the white swans that already consume their time, but prepare for more black (and grey) swans that will emerge with little or no warning. There will be plenty of new threats, but emerging technologies and increasing cyber connectedness also bring opportunities for Australian agencies to collect information on, influence and counter our intelligence adversaries, both at home and abroad. ∎

DRAWING THE LINE

Witness K and the ethics of spying

Kim McGrath

In the first week of January 2019, a private jet landed at Presidente Nicolau Lobato International Airport in Dili, the capital of Timor-Leste. Former Victorian premier Steve Bracks emerged into the monsoonal heat and was greeted by staff from the office of Xanana Gusmão, Timor-Leste's chief maritime boundary negotiator. They drove Bracks to the waterfront café at the Novo Turismo Resort and Spa, where Gusmão was waiting. The subject of the meeting was Bernard Collaery, Gusmão's former lawyer, who was pleading not guilty to breaches of Australia's intelligence act.

Collaery's charges related to an Australian Secret Intelligence Service (ASIS) operation in Dili in 2004, in which Canberra is believed to have recorded Timor-Leste officials' private discussions about maritime boundary negotiations with Australia. In 2013, the Australian government revealed the allegations of spying.

Five years later, in June 2018, Attorney-General Christian Porter consented to charges being laid against Collaery and a retired ASIS agent known only as Witness K for "conspiring to reveal classified information".

Gusmão led the Timorese resistance against the Indonesian occupation in the mountains of East Timor and, after his capture in 1992, from his jail cell in Jakarta. In 2002, he became Timor-Leste's first president, and later served as its prime minister.

Bracks says Gusmão wanted to know what he could do to support Collaery, who had been his lawyer following Timor's independence from Indonesia in 1999 and on several subsequent occasions.

> Gusmão saw it as a moral issue. He said he would travel to Canberra if necessary, to give evidence in support of Collaery and Witness K, because, he told me, it would be against his conscience not to. He saw them as "honourable men" who should have been lauded for their actions. From his viewpoint, they had revealed a crime. A crime against one of the poorest countries in the world, by one of the richest.

In April 2020, the Supreme Court of the Australian Capital Territory was due to hold a preliminary hearing about the extent to which Collaery's case would be heard in public. Gusmão was planning to go to Canberra to give evidence, until COVID-19 travel restrictions led to the hearing date being vacated. Witness K's plea date was also postponed. Collaery's hearing was re-listed for May. The hearing was held in secret, so it is unknown if Gusmão's evidence was tendered or if he appeared by video link.

The prosecution of Collaery and Witness K throws a spotlight on the nexus between politics and intelligence, and the unfettered power of ministers in Australia's intelligence regime. Unfortunately for Collaery and Witness K, and the 7000 staff currently working in Australia's ten intelligence agencies, it also shows that opportunities for an operative to challenge a direction to perform an immoral or illegal act are limited and likely to be career-ending.

"People in ASIS are not devoid of conscience ... but there is no avenue for them to raise concerns."

According to section 11 of the *Intelligence Services Act 2001*, ASIS and the other five agencies to which the Act applies are to work "only in the interests of Australia's national security, Australia's foreign relations or Australia's national economic well-being". Australians accept the need for extreme secrecy around spying operations aimed at combatting terrorism and other security threats. But does that social licence extend to using espionage for illegal, immoral or corrupt acts? Should the state use its spies against a friendly government for purely economic gain, either for the state or for private companies?

Leading security analyst Desmond Ball warned that "the relationship between intelligence and policy is complex and delicate.

It can easily become politicized, so demeaning the intelligence process and ultimately risking national security." This is what happened in Canberra in 2004–05. And it is arguably what drove Witness K to later raise with the Inspector-General of Intelligence and Security (IGIS) disquiet within ASIS about the operation.

The office of the IGIS is responsible for ensuring Australia's intelligence agencies act "legally and with propriety, comply with ministerial guidelines and directives and respect human rights". In early 2008, Witness K approached the IGIS, Ian Carnell, alleging that a cultural change within ASIS had led to his constructive dismissal. According to a statement Collaery made to federal parliament, part of the complaint involved an operation Witness K "had been ordered to execute in Dili, Timor-Leste". Carnell allowed Witness K to take private legal action, but this could only be done through a lawyer with the security clearance to act for intelligence agents. Collaery was on a list of such lawyers. Despite his well-known connections with the Timorese leadership and the fact that Witness K's grievance involved the Dili operation, Collaery was appointed Witness K's lawyer.

Collaery is restricted by national security legislation from talking about the operation. Clinton Fernandes, an Australian Intelligence Corps officer from 1997 to 2006 now at the University of New South Wales, is not so constrained. In his 2018 book *Island off the Coast of Asia*, Fernandes writes that the listening devices installed in the Palácio do Governo were turned on and off by a covert agent inside the building. They then beamed the recording by microwave signal to a line-of-sight covert listening base set up inside the Central Maritime Hotel … The digital recordings were then allegedly couriered across town to the Australian embassy, and sent to Canberra for analysis.

The 127-room Central Maritime Hotel was a converted Russian hospital ship that was rebuilt in Finland, used as a hotel in Myanmar and then towed to Dili because there were no hotels or restaurants of suitable standard for international visitors. It was conveniently moored opposite the waterfront white-stuccoed Palácio do Governo.

The 2005 Commission for Reception, Truth and Reconciliation in East Timor estimated that more than 150,000 people, a quarter of the population, were murdered or deliberately starved to death between 1974 and 1999, when the territory was under Indonesian rule – a brutal occupation aided and abetted by Australia. In 2004, when the Dili bugging occurred, the Timorese remained physically and emotionally traumatised. Of the 177 countries on the United Nations Development Programme Human Development Index measuring poverty, Timor-Leste languished at 158, one place above Rwanda.

Retired diplomat Bruce Haigh says ASIS officers involved in the Dili operation were put in an impossible position: "People in ASIS are not devoid of conscience. I've known many ASIS and ASIO officers over the years … They want to keep Australia, and Australians, safe. They would object to such an immoral operation, but there is no

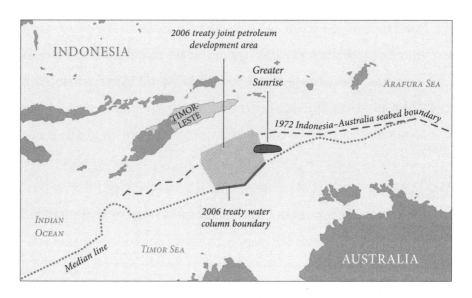

The Greater Sunrise oil and gas fields, which lie in the Timor Sea between Australia and Timor-Leste, were the cause of a long and controversial dispute between the two neighbours.

avenue for them to raise concerns." Former ASIS spy Warren Reed argues that most intelligence officers have "a keen sense" of democratic values and "will generally stand firm against attempts by their service's management to diverge from those widely accepted norms of behaviour".

The current director-general of ASIS, Paul Symon, has stressed that ASIS acts only in response to a list of priorities set out by the National Security Committee (NSC), chaired by the prime minister. ASIS reports to the minister for foreign affairs, also a member of the NSC, who must authorise specific activities. In 2004, that minister was Alexander Downer.

When the operation became public in 2013, Downer, long retired from politics, defended Australia's tactics in the Timor Sea negotiations. He told the ABC's *Four Corners* program in March 2014 that he could not confirm or deny the spying. But he added: "The Australian government was on Australia's side in the negotiations and we did our best to make sure that we were able to achieve our objective."

Australia's objective was to retain rights to hydrocarbon-rich areas of the Timor Sea much closer to Timor than to Australia. In the early 1960s, Australia issued petroleum exploration permits in the Timor Sea to Woodside, now Australia's largest natural gas producer, in areas contested

De Mello reported Downer told him "Australia could bring meltdown to East Timor if it so chose".

by Indonesia and Portuguese Timor. Australia refused Portugal's requests for talks and instead negotiated a treaty with Indonesia in 1972. The agreed boundary skirted the edges of the permits issued to Woodside and other companies – well north of the median line.

Woodside discovered the Greater Sunrise oil and gas fields in 1974. The following year, with Australia's covert support, Indonesia invaded Portuguese Timor. Unlike Portugal, which had argued for a median-line boundary, Indonesia suggested joining the end points of the 1972 treaty, which would have put Greater Sunrise entirely in Australian waters. Despite UN resolutions calling on Indonesia to withdraw, Australia commenced negotiations with Indonesia in 1979 to agree on a boundary between Australia and occupied East Timor. This amounted to Australia formally recognising Indonesia's sovereignty in Timor, the only Western nation to do so.

However, once negotiations commenced, Indonesia argued for a median line. It took a decade to reach agreement on the Timor Gap Treaty, infamously signed by foreign ministers Gareth Evans and Ali Alatas in a jet as they drank champagne over the Timor Sea in December 1989. The treaty established a "resource-sharing arrangement" (not a permanent boundary) that gave Australia rights to the lucrative oil and gas fields off the coast of East Timor.

By the late 1990s, the possibility of an independent East Timor was threatening the treaty. If East Timor became independent, the deal Australia had negotiated with the illegal occupier would cease to exist. East Timor would have rights under the United Nations Convention on the Law of the Sea, ratified by Australia in 1994, including the right to a 200-nautical-mile exclusive economic zone (EEZ). The Timor Sea is approximately 350 nautical miles wide, so Australia and East Timor would have overlapping EEZ entitlements. The boundary would be determined by international law, and would likely involve drawing an equidistant line halfway between the coasts of neighbouring states.

Downer worked hard to keep the Timor Gap Treaty alive, even before East Timor gained independence. A month after Indonesia's surprise January 1999 agreement to a vote of self-determination in

East Timor, Downer visited Jakarta and sought out Xanana Gusmão, who was under house arrest after six years in Indonesia's top-security prison, Cipinang.

Downer talked to Gusmão about, among other things, the smooth transition of the Timor Gap Treaty from Indonesia to East Timor. In an interview with filmmaker Gil Scrine in Dili in March 2019, Gusmão said he was surprised that the Australian foreign minister wanted to talk about the treaty. He recalled telling Downer that he was not "prepared to talk about oil and gas" and instead pleaded for international troops to quell the escalating violence.

In October 2000, Sérgio Vieira de Mello, head of the United Nations Transitional Administration in East Timor (UNTAET), met with Downer and other ministers in Canberra and was also surprised that their "key preoccupation" was the treaty. Amid the deployment of more than 5500 Australian personnel in East Timor, and the massive development challenge facing the Timorese people, Canberra's focus was on the energy resources in the Timor Sea. De Mello cabled a colleague after the meetings that the Timor Sea issue "elicited a strong – even strident – reaction from Downer and his department". De Mello reported Downer told him "Australia could bring meltdown to East Timor if it so chose".

Between July 2001 and April 2003, Downer made four trips to Dili. Initially his aim was to ask UNTAET to step into Indonesia's shoes and accept the terms of the Timor Gap Treaty. This was a big request, as Australia's claim beyond the median line was as belligerent and out of step with the UN Convention on the Law of the Sea as China's nine-dash line in the South China Sea. Australia's diplomacy also risked alienating a friendly, desperately poor neighbour that was the subject of a massive international effort to establish statehood.

UNTAET's negotiators pushed back, arguing for a boundary reflecting international law – a median line and lateral boundaries that would put all of Greater Sunrise in Timorese waters. But the UN negotiating team was under-resourced and overworked – and, for all we know, Australia's intelligence agencies may have also been secretly lending assistance to Australia's negotiators.

Two months before Timor-Leste's independence, and just weeks after an American company, Oceanic Exploration, offered to fund a Timorese application to the International Court of Justice to determine the maritime boundary, Australia withdrew from the jurisdiction of the International Tribunal for the Law of the Sea and the maritime division of the ICJ. In a media release on 25 March 2002, Downer stated, "Australia's strong view is that any maritime boundary dispute is best settled by negotiation rather than litigation."

UNTAET had some small victories, but when the Democratic Republic of Timor-Leste came into existence on 20 May 2002, its first official act was to sign the heads of agreement for the 2002 Timor Sea Treaty with Australia. Modelled on the Timor Gap Treaty, this created a revenue-sharing arrangement, not a maritime boundary, and left 80 per cent of Greater Sunrise outside the "Joint Petroleum Development Area". It was a huge win for Australia.

In November 2003, 100 international non-government organisations signed a letter to John Howard, criticising Australia's "callous" approach and warning that its long-term interests were "best served by a stable and prosperous East Timor". The Howard government had a different assessment of Australia's interests. It considered the possibility of Timor-Leste gaining sovereignty to the median line in the Timor Sea such a threat "to Australia's national security, foreign relations or economic well-being" that it was apparently necessary to direct ASIS (and possibly other intelligence agencies) to support Australia's negotiating team. This was a damning indictment of Australia's negotiators, some of the best and brightest lawyers in government, backed by the resources of multiple departments. Timor-Leste's team was led by former US ambassador Peter Galbraith, supported by a handful of idealistic young lawyers.

Timor-Leste asked for a 50–50 share of Greater Sunrise. Australia refused

One of the issues that reportedly drove Witness K to complain to the IGIS was his concern that intelligence assets were being diverted from the war on terror to the Dili operation. The Timor Sea negotiations started in 2004, just three years after al-Qaeda terrorists ploughed passenger jets into the twin towers in New York on 11 September 2001. Following the attack, Howard invoked the ANZUS Treaty and committed Australia to support "United States–led action against those responsible for these tragic attacks". This resulted in Australia's participation in wars in Afghanistan and Iraq, heightening the security threat in Australia and increasing pressure on its intelligence assets.

A year after September 11, Downer told parliament that the government had received information "about a generic threat to Australian and United Nations interests in South-East Asia". At the time, more than 20,000 Australian tourists visited the Indonesian island of Bali each month. Three days after Downer's statement, DFAT amended its travel advice for Indonesia but, in bold type, stated that services were "operating normally" in Bali.

This was a catastrophic failure of Australian intelligence. On 12 October 2002, two members of Jemaah Islamiyah, a South-East Asian extremist Islamist group with links to al-Qaeda, set off bombs in the Sari nightclub and Paddy's Bar at Kuta Beach in Bali, killing 202 people, including 88 Australians and 38 Indonesians. Days later, the Howard government was forced to admit that two weeks before the blasts, it had received a US intelligence report that included Bali among targets for an impending terrorist attack. Howard told parliament that the report was analysed by Australian intelligence assessors, who decided that travel warnings did not need to be upgraded. Applying the narrowest definition of "intelligence", Howard insisted he had been assured there was no specific information warning of an attack on 12 October in Bali. The IGIS came to the same self-serving conclusion. Warren Reed said it was "an unthinkable and unforgivable failure of the intelligence network".

In July 2004, the Howard government released a white paper on terrorism. In the foreword, Downer wrote that the government was responding to the threat with a "sustained and strategic campaign". ASIO and ASIS budgets had been boosted, the paper noted, because intelligence offered "the best chance of detecting terrorist activity and allowing us to take steps to prevent an attack". Jemaah Islamiyah was named as a key threat.

Two months later, Jemaah Islamiyah claimed responsibility when a car bomb exploded in the driveway of the Australian embassy in Jakarta. In addition to the suicide bomber, eight people were killed, including the embassy gardener and four Indonesian police, and more than 150 wounded.

A month after that, in October 2004, the Dili bugging operation reportedly commenced during the second round of boundary negotiations between Australia and Timor-Leste. Despite the ASIS budget expansion, officers with the technical skills to install listening devices in the cabinet room of a foreign country were in short supply. As Fernandes explains, installation is a delicate operation. "You need physical access to the room, so you have to invent a plausible story. Then you have to map the geometry of the office, check the acoustics, work out where to place the listening devices, and because it's going to go on for several weeks or months, you need a power source." And in this case, where the cover story involved renovating the government offices under the guise of an Australian aid program, ASIS needed skilled tradespeople to carry out the renovations.

At the first substantive round of boundary talks in Dili in April 2004, Timor-Leste argued that international law meant there should be a median line boundary. Australia refused to consider changes to the boundaries in the Timor Gap Treaty. A breakthrough came in August, after a meeting in Canberra between Downer and Timor-Leste's foreign minister, José Ramos-Horta. They reached a "creative solution" in which Australia would accept Timor-Leste's claim outside the Joint Petroleum Development Area. How Timor-Leste would be recompensed was still to be resolved. This took some of the heat out of the issue in the lead-up to Australia's federal election in October, which the Coalition won.

A bevy of senior DFAT officials attended the next round of talks in Dili in October 2004. Timor-Leste asked for a 50–50 share of Greater Sunrise. Australia refused and instead put A$3 billion on the table with a deadline. Timor-Leste rejected the offer. The talks ended in acrimony.

Yet by May 2005, a deal had been reached. It was presumably in the lead-up to this deal that Australia took advantage of the recordings of Timor-Leste's negotiating team. It is also likely the bugging was not the only action Australia's intelligence agencies took to assist the negotiators. In an article in *The Australian* in 2013, Paul Cleary, an adviser to the Timor-Leste government during the negotiations, recalled that senior members of Timor-Leste's negotiating team "believed one of their members was turned by ASIS during the 2004–05 negotiations over Greater Sunrise". In his book *Shakedown*,

Cleary remembered Australia's negotiators "hinted at Australia's monitoring of internet use by East Timor's advisers". Tom Clarke, who coordinated the Melbourne-based Timor Sea Justice Campaign, says there was a three-month period in early 2005, when the campaign was at its height, in which he suspected his mobile phone was bugged. "My phone was making all sorts of weird noises and doing strange things. I was receiving recordings of my own phone conversations in my own message bank."

The Treaty on Certain Maritime Arrangements in the Timor Sea (CMATS) was signed in January 2006 by foreign ministers Downer and Ramos-Horta. It set up a "resource-sharing arrangement" like the Timor Gap Treaty

The Timorese "knew they'd been dudded, they just didn't know how"

and copied that treaty's boundaries. Eighty per cent of Greater Sunrise was outside the boundary. A draconian clause banned permanent maritime boundary negotiations for fifty years (unless oil and gas reserves were depleted earlier). In return, Timor-Leste got an ongoing 50 per cent interest in revenue from Greater Sunrise. An innocuous-sounding clause provided that if there was no approved development plan by 23 February 2013, the treaty could be terminated by either party.

While CMATS was publicly applauded as a win by both nations, it was in fact another major victory for Australia, given international law clearly favoured a median-line boundary. As Collaery told

Steve Bracks in April 2020, the Timorese "knew they'd been dudded, they just didn't know how".

Fernandes observes that "spy agencies have relied for many years on nonofficial cover within certain companies with foreign operations, with the knowledge and consent of a tiny minority of their directors". It is of course unknown if this has ever been the case at Woodside. There has, however, been a close relationship between the company, DFAT and Australian politicians from both major parties. Ashton Calvert, secretary of DFAT at the time of the bugging operation, joined the Woodside board eight months after retiring from the department in January 2005. The chair of Woodside was prominent Liberal Party fundraiser Charles Goode. In 2010, Woodside employed former DFAT officer Brendan Augustin as country manager in Dili. This seemed a strange move, as Augustin's past with DFAT was known in Timor, and his appointment only confirmed suspicions that Woodside and DFAT were acting hand in glove. A 2008 investigation by *The Age* found it was Woodside's corporate affairs director, Gary Gray, who suggested recruiting from DFAT when Augustin was hired to work for the company in 2006. After leaving Woodside in 2007, Gray went on to become minister for resources and energy in the Gillard Labor government.

Despite the 2006 treaty, there was still conflict between Australia and Timor-Leste about where the gas from Greater Sunrise would be processed. Timor-Leste was determined to see the gas processed on its south coast. Australia wanted it processed in Darwin.

Woodside was pushing for a floating plant.

In mid-2008, Downer resigned from parliament after the Coalition lost the 2007 election. He founded a lobbying company, Bespoke Approach, and Woodside signed on as a client. Downer's relationship with Woodside post-parliament was reportedly another reason Witness K was prompted to raise his concerns about the Dili operation with the IGIS.

Woodside and Downer clearly did not know that Gusmão was by then aware of the bugging and Downer's likely role in approving it. Gusmão told Bracks that he was briefed on the operation in Darwin in 2008. Clearly a master of the long game, he decided to sit on the information until February 2013, when CMATS's trigger date for termination was imminent and a new treaty could potentially be negotiated.

The Australian ambassador in Dili, Miles Armitage, eventually secured a "courtesy" meeting for Downer with a reluctant Gusmão. Downer passed on a message from Woodside's managing director, Don Voelte, that the company would offer significant development money if Gusmão dropped the option of a pipeline to Timor. Gusmão refused.

In November 2012, with the CMATS trigger date approaching, Gusmão moved. During talks between Timor-Leste, Indonesia and Australia in Bali, he raised privately with Julia Gillard, then Australia's prime minister, that there was a problem they needed to quietly resolve. Gusmão proposed a political dialogue with the Australian government about the spying, and a renegotiation of the treaty, using the February 2013 trigger. He aimed to keep the bugging confidential, protecting the international reputation of Australia and ASIS.

On 7 December 2012, Timor-Leste's foreign minister hand-delivered Gillard a letter from Gusmão and an aide-mémoire requesting discussions regarding the invalidity of CMATS. According to Collaery in his book, *Oil Under Troubled Water*, it was agreed with Gillard that the issue would remain confidential. Gillard sent a message back denying the substance of the complaint and compounded the problem by sending Margaret Twomey, the ambassador in Dili at the time of the alleged undercover operation, to meet with Gusmão on her behalf. Gusmão was incredulous. Faced with the Australian government's denial of the bugging, Gusmão initiated confidential proceedings in the Permanent Court of Arbitration in The Hague, seeking to have CMATS declared void because Australia had acted in bad faith by spying during the negotiations. Witness K was to be Timor-Leste's lead witness.

Oddly, it was the Gillard government that made the spying allegations public. On 3 May 2013, foreign minister Bob Carr and attorney-general Mark Dreyfus issued a statement advising that Timor-Leste had initiated arbitration:

Timor-Leste argues that … Australia did not conduct the CMATS negotiations in 2004 in good faith by engaging in espionage … Australia has always conducted itself in a professional manner in diplomatic negotiations and conducted the CMATS treaty negotiations in good faith.

ABC Radio Darwin reported on the statement, but the dispute was ignored by the national media until Leo Shanahan published a story in *The Australian* on 29 May 2013. According to the article, "Downer directly authorised the operation to listen covertly to the negotiations in a cabinet room built with Australian aid".

In September, the Coalition, led by Tony Abbott, won the federal election. In December, ASIO and the Australian Federal Police (AFP) executed a search warrant on Collaery's home and chambers, issued by Attorney-General George Brandis under powers given after September 11 to combat terrorism. David Irvine, the director-general of ASIS at the time of the Dili maritime boundary negotiations, was then director-general of

There is very limited parliamentary scrutiny of Australia's intelligence agencies

ASIO. Witness K's home was simultaneously raided and his passport confiscated.

The raids occurred on the eve of the arbitration proceedings at The Hague. They succeeded in making Australia's spying on its impoverished neighbour front-page news around the world, and prompted questions about the ethics and legitimacy of Australia's intelligence agencies. Timor-Leste immediately challenged Australia's actions in the International Court of Justice. An interim hearing at the ICJ resulted in Australia being ordered to seal the documents and not to spy on Timor's lawyers pending a full hearing at a later date. This was an internationally humiliating outcome for Australia. In June 2015, after Australia returned the seized documents, Timor-Leste discontinued the ICJ case.

In February 2014, when whistleblower Edward Snowden revealed that the Defence Signals Directorate, now the Australian Signals Directorate, spied on an American law firm representing Indonesia in a trade dispute with the United States, Prime Minister Abbott insisted Australia did not spy for commercial purposes. He told ABC Radio:

> I don't comment on this kind of allegation, but the fact is we don't collect intelligence for commercial purposes. We collect intelligence to save Australian lives, to save the lives of Australian people, to promote Australian values, to promote the universal decencies of humanity and to help our friends and neighbours, including Indonesia ... our intelligence has been instrumental in defending many terrorist attacks in Indonesia and elsewhere.

In April 2016, with the arbitration stalled because Witness K could not travel without a passport, Timor-Leste sought to bring Australia to the negotiating table by invoking untested compulsory conciliation provisions of the UN Convention on the Law of the Sea. Australia challenged the jurisdiction of the commission, losing on all six grounds. In January 2017, following a series of meetings with the conciliation commission, a joint statement by the two countries announced that Australia had accepted Timor-Leste's termination of CMATS and had agreed to negotiate permanent boundaries. The quid pro quo became public a fortnight later in another joint statement that revealed Timor-Leste had dropped the embarrassing spying arbitration in a show of good faith and "in continuation of the confidence-building measures".

The end result was a Timor Sea boundary that essentially followed a median line and gave Timor-Leste 80 per cent of Greater Sunrise if the gas is processed in Darwin or 70 per cent if processed in Timor. The treaty was signed at the United Nations in New York in March 2018. This was the outcome the Howard government was desperate to avoid in the negotiations more than a decade earlier – so desperate that it allegedly diverted intelligence assets from the war on terror to assist Australia's negotiating team in Dili.

The Dili spying operation shamed Australia to the negotiating table. It focused attention on Australia's hypocritical criticism of China's South China Sea claims and made a mockery of Australia's backing of the "international rules-based order". The resolution of the dispute meant that for the first time since Timor-Leste's independence, the Australia – Timor-Leste relationship was not poisoned by the conflict. As Timor-Leste's minister of state, Ágio Pereira, told a reception after the signing ceremony, the treaty marked a "new chapter in the bilateral relationship".

But instead of moving to cement this new beginning, in June 2018, four months after the treaty signing, five years after the Dili bugging operation became public and fourteen years after it occurred, the attorney-general, Christian Porter, in what was now the Morrison-led Coalition government, consented to charges being laid against Collaery and Witness K.

This sent a chilling message. In Australia, it confirmed that the government will not tolerant dissent, and had few regrets about an exploitative operation against a friendly neighbour. In Timor-Leste, it was seen as yet another betrayal.

What options are there when the direction to perform an immoral act comes from a minister or the NSC? Since January 2014, Australian public servants, ASIS agents included, have had the right to raise suspected wrongdoing under the *Public Interest Disclosure Act 2013*. The Act provides that ASIS officers can make a disclosure to the IGIS. They cannot, however, disclose "the proper performance of [the] functions and proper exercise of [the] powers" of an intelligence agency or its officials. This raises the question: who determines what is proper? If the minister gave the direction for the operation, it would take a brave IGIS to find it improper.

There is very limited parliamentary scrutiny of Australia's intelligence agencies. Coalition governments gave the directions for the Dili spying, the ASIO and AFP raids on Collaery and Witness K, and the decision to prosecute them, yet the Labor Party has remained largely silent. Centre Alliance senator Rex Patrick has called for the Parliamentary Joint Committee on Intelligence and Security (PJCIS) to be reformed in line with the Canadian model, allowing it to review intelligence policy, procedures and coordination, so long as this will not threaten ongoing operations, national security or foreign relations. Patrick put a private member's bill along these lines to the Senate in 2018. It was rejected as "premature" because Dennis Richardson, director-general of ASIO from 1996 to 2005 and later secretary of defence and DFAT, had been commissioned to conduct a "comprehensive review of the legal framework governing the national intelligence community". A declassified version of Richardson's review has not yet been released.

Australia's intelligence agencies are perennially in review or restructure. The one constant is the small pool of senior officials who rotate around the director-general and departmental secretary positions. The 2017 Independent Intelligence Review was conducted by Michael L'Estrange and Stephen Merchant. L'Estrange was a policy adviser to the Liberal Party before being appointed secretary of cabinet and then secretary of DFAT from 2005 to 2009. Merchant was director of the Defence Signals Directorate from 2002 to 2006 and then a senior official in the defence department and DFAT. They recommended a restructure and rebranding of some of Australia's intelligence agencies, generous budget increases and granting the PJCIS the power to initiate inquiries into administrative and budget matters. However, on "the legality and propriety

The consolidation of power in the Home Affairs portfolio was a purely political decision

of particular operational activities", the best they could propose was a referral to the IGIS.

The same day their review was released to the public, then prime minister Malcom Turnbull surprised L'Estrange and Merchant by announcing the establishment of the Department of Home Affairs – a reform not among their recommendations. ASIO and the AFP were transferred from the Attorney-General's Department to Home Affairs, and the IGIS from the Department of the Prime Minister and Cabinet to the Attorney-General's. The consolidation of power in Peter Dutton's Home Affairs portfolio was a purely political decision, as Turnbull makes clear in his autobiography.

In a submission to the Richardson review, security analysts Anthony Bergin and Kate Grayson argue the IGIS should be "transferred back to PM&C, where it sat since its foundation, to help guarantee its complete independence as an oversight body". They also call for the PJCIS to have the power to analyse the operations of intelligence agencies and to conduct its own inquiries. They argue that while the IGIS oversees the activities of intelligence agencies, "it doesn't focus on whether they should be conducting those activities". The Dili bugging is a glaring example of an operation that should have been reviewed by the PJCIS.

Tom Clarke, now director of campaigns at the Human Rights Law Centre, suggests removing the "economic well-being" element from section 11 of the *Intelligence Services Act 2001* "so Australian agents are never again used for such morally bankrupt purposes". He argues that what is "most upsetting about Australia spying on Timor-Leste was that it was not about national security – it was about economic gain". Clarke's view is echoed by the Law Council of Australia, which argues that including economic well-being in the definition of national security may allow intelligence agencies to use their powers on "a wide range of issues that are disproportionate to their purpose". But reform is unlikely, as it was the Labor government that in 2011 amended the Act to add "economic well-being" as a rationale for spying.

Peter Edwards – historian and biographer of Justice Robert Hope, the architect of Australia's intelligence system – has called for the next Independent Intelligence Review, due around 2022, to be upgraded to a royal commission in order to enable a complete "reassessment of the structures, legislation and operations of the whole intelligence community". He argues that the COVID-19 crisis has shown that national security, and related concepts such as intelligence, must be redefined to include health, environmental and other non-traditional threats, as well as long-term economic security.

A royal commission cannot come soon enough. The first term of reference should be to enquire into the circumstances that led to the Dili bugging and any concurrent intelligence operations that were designed to exploit a vulnerable neighbour, while the war on terror was threatening Australian lives at home and abroad. ■

PARTY FAITHFUL

How China spies –
and how to resist

Anne-Marie Brady

China has the world's largest spy network, but its approach to intelligence has one crucial difference from that of other states. It has separate intelligence units that belong either to the party, the state or the military – and the core task of all is to maintain Chinese Community Party (CCP) rule. This diverges from intelligence agencies in liberal democracies, whose purpose is not to support one political party or leader but to focus on national security. The CCP's broad-ranging approach to covert activities, which makes extensive use of assets, disinformation and proxies, makes its foreign spying and political interference challenging to combat with traditional counter-intelligence measures. Add in decades of post–Cold War complacency, arrogance about the superiority of liberal democracies over communist systems, and cutbacks in the public sector, and the Western targets of CCP espionage are revealed as unaware and underprepared.

After September 11, many Western intelligence agencies focused almost exclusively on counterterrorism. NATO states also continued to focus on the threat from Russia. But most foreign nations, institutions and businesses have only recently begun to address concerns about China's covert intelligence-gathering and surveillance activities.

The resources and expertise to assess and address Chinese espionage is alarmingly thin across the Five Eyes network and its partners. China conducts in-depth studies of its foreign adversaries, even tracking the attitudes and statements of individual China watchers in Western countries. However, the targets of this surveillance often lack basic knowledge about the organisational structure of the CCP intelligence system. For example, in a speech in February 2020, US secretary of state Mike Pompeo told US governors that the Chinese People's Association for Friendship with Foreign Countries (commonly known as the Friendship Association, or Youxie), which had compiled dossiers on them and their attitudes to China, "is the public face of the Chinese Communist Party's official foreign influence agency, the United Front Work Department". Actually, the Friendship Association has three "mothers-in-law" (to use CCP parlance): the Ministry of Foreign Affairs, the Chinese People's Political Consultative Conference – which is affiliated with the United Front Work Department – and the International Liaison Department. The Friendship Association, like all CCP agencies and affiliates, engages in united front work, but it is not "the public face of the United Front

Work Department". It was a telling error from Pompeo, who, before joining the White House, was the director of the CIA.

Veteran Jesuit China watcher Father László Ladány once remarked that the People's Republic of China (PRC) was based on a triple foundation: ideology, the power of the party and the secret police. In essence he was paraphrasing Mao Zedong, who championed the CCP's three magic weapons: ideological discipline, the military and underground activities – what the CCP calls united front work. The CCP recognised early on the necessity of intelligence and espionage in achieving its political agenda. Mao and other revolutionary leaders honed their asymmetric warfare skills during the Chinese Civil War and then during the PRC's international isolation from 1949 to 1971. Mao also used the security agencies in his struggle for dominance within the CCP, and then later turned against some of their most senior leaders.

As the CCP leadership's ambitions have increased, so has the significance of Chinese intelligence activities in the contest for global power. The COVID-19 pandemic has both posed a risk to China's power and allowed opportunities to extend it. A report by the China Institutes of Contemporary International Relations, an intelligence think tank affiliated with China's Ministry of State Security, has warned that the PRC's attempt to cover up the early stages of the epidemic and corner global supplies of personal protective equipment, such as masks, made China politically weak and risked global pushback against its agenda. The Xi government has tried to seize control of the global narrative on

COVID-19 and has tightly censored information about the situation in China, while also aggressively promoting disinformation internationally. The Chinese military has taken advantage of other countries' focus on containing COVID-19 to assert its position in the South China Sea, India, Taiwan and Hong Kong with shows of force. The FBI reported that China has launched cyberattacks against US COVID-19 research facilities. China's political interference against foreign governments during the pandemic has become increasingly brazen. And it has used economic coercion to intimidate states such as Australia, which have spoken up for Taiwan at the World Health Organization and asked for an international inquiry into the origins of COVID-19. China's

China has more professional intelligence agents operating overseas than any other country

multiple intelligence agencies have played a role in all these actions.

A nexus of party, state, military and market

While there is a plethora of books and articles on US and Russian intelligence agencies, little is known publicly about the many organisations involved in China's intelligence-gathering, surveillance and espionage. This helps to keep its activities in foreign countries under the radar and assists in plausible deniability.

For anyone interested in contemporary geopolitics, it is essential to understand the CCP and how it rules China. CCP literacy requires learning the ABCs of China's intelligence agencies and their role in politics. The Xi government's covert operations draw on the resources of the CCP, the People's Liberation Army (PLA) and the private sector in China, as well as Chinese companies abroad, what I call the party-state-military-market nexus. The most infamous example of these relationships is Huawei Technologies, which has extremely close links to the PLA and the Ministry of State Security, while its owner-ship structure of employee trade union members puts it squarely within the CCP United Front Work Department.

Through this nexus, China has a vast number of personnel engaged in intelligence-gathering, counterintelligence and espionage, and has more professional intelligence agents operating overseas than any other country, from sleeper agents to those sent abroad for short missions. Chinese intelligence agencies frequently use academic conferences, business meetings, government exchanges and "study tours" for CCP officials as covers for agents to visit a country. Think-tank partnerships, city-to-city "friendship" links (which are run by the Chinese People's Association for Friendship with Foreign Countries) and proxy diaspora organisations are also utilised. CCP intelligence operatives have always cooperated with secret societies, triads and criminal gangs, too. Indeed, in 1990, the then doyen of China watchers, Pierre Ryckmans, observed that the CCP "is in essence a secret society. In its methods and mentality it presents a striking resemblance to an underworld mob".

In the PRC, as in the Soviet Union, the legal system is a means to control the population through "rule by law" rather than rule of law. In 2017, China introduced national intelligence legislation that requires all Chinese citizens and companies, as well as foreigners and foreign companies operating in China, to cooperate with and support China's intelligence-gathering activities by granting access to information as requested. This simply codified existing practices. CCP intelligence agencies have historically used tactics of blackmail, bribery, exploiting psychological weaknesses and other forms of coercion to develop asset relationships. Ideology is much less a motivator for cooperation than might be supposed.

CCP intelligence agencies make significant use of civilian assets and proxies – an approach that has often been described as "mosaic", while some use the term "a thousand grains of sand". However, Peter Mattis, a leading author on China's intelligence services, has warned that these concepts risk implicating a vast amount of China-connected activity that may not be related to espionage. It also, he notes, underestimates the activities of China's professional spies – who are numerous even without the help of civilian assets.

Those participating in CCP espionage are a tiny percentage of the overall Chinese population. The majority of China's citizens at home and in the Chinese diaspora are the victims of CCP control efforts. It is important to distinguish between the party-state and its people. They should not be lumped together as "the Chinese" – as some politicians and journalists outside China tend to do. This only plays into CCP narratives that label any criticism of its policies as "xenophobia", "racial prejudice", "demonising China", "Cold War thinking" and "McCarthyism".

The Xi era

Unlike most other nations' spy agencies, Chinese intelligence organisations are highly politicised. They are tasked with monitoring the Chinese population as much as the outside world. Intelligence personnel, like most of those who hold sensitive positions in China, are almost always CCP members. Their loyalty is to the CCP, and to individual leaders within the CCP, not to Chinese society.

Understanding the CCP's intelligence agenda requires engaging with the Party's Marxist-Leninist-Maoist, and now also Xi-ist, worldview. This perspective is not hard to locate: promoting the CCP political message is a key task of the domestic media, the so-called "tongue and throat" of the Party. It is not possible to understand the CCP and its policies unless you read its documents, preferably in Chinese. Surprisingly, this is still rare among China watchers.

The CCP sorts all government agencies and activities into groupings known as *xitong*. The state intelligence agencies are part of the politics and law *xitong*, under the leadership of Guo Shengkun. Guo ultimately reports to Xi, who heads the National Security Commission, which oversees all the agencies within China's intelligence sector, as well as many others with a national security function.

Guo's predecessor, Zhou Yongkang, was a member of the Politburo Standing Committee, the top governing body of China, but he was accused of plotting a coup just before Xi became general secretary in 2012. Guo sits on the twenty-five-member Politburo, but is not part of its the Standing Committee, which consists of the top seven leaders, and his lower status likely reflects this history. Guo, like Zhou Yongkang, is affiliated with the Jiang Zemin (former CCP general secretary) faction within the CCP, which has many senior figures in China's security organisations.

The PLA is the party's military, not the state's. It has parallel structures to the CCP organs for information management and senior appointments, the Central Propaganda Department and the Central Organisation Department. PLA intelligence organisations are under the

Xi has been able to steadily place his people at the top of all the core intelligence agencies

direct leadership of Xi, as he heads the Central Military Commission. External-facing intelligence services are part of the foreign affairs *xitong*, also led by Xi, as head of the Central Foreign Affairs Commission. Xi heads the Central Leading Group for Taiwan Affairs, too. As general secretary of the CCP, Xi also supervises CCP organisations with an intelligence function, such as the United Front Work Department and the International Liaison Department.

Xi is the most powerful CCP leader in the past forty years, and his ability to steadily place his people at the top of all the core intelligence agencies, as well as the propaganda and thought work *xitong*, is a mark of his political strength. Even so, this is not a guarantee of absolute control of the security agencies. Xi's rivals in the CCP have seeded these agencies from top to bottom with their allies. The intelligence organisations operate independently, even though their heads report to Xi. Yet no other senior CCP leader has had this much control over the PRC security agencies since Mao.

In the Mao, Deng, Jiang and Hu eras, there was a considerable degree of stovepiping and institutional and factional rivalries among the CCP's spy agencies. Leadership structures were more diffuse, and key decisions were made by consensus. Today, Xi's position at the top of multiple intelligence-related *xitong* means there is a higher level of coordination on covert activities.

Xi has instituted major reforms that have further consolidated his power. One of the largest changes was the establishment of the National Security Commission. At its first meeting in 2014, Xi stated that China faced three great threats: invasion, subversion and division. The Xi administration uses intelligence collection, counterintelligence and espionage to counter these threats, which it views as both domestic and external.

Xi had early exposure to both the CCP and military intelligence systems in his first job after graduating from Qinghua University. From 1979 to 1982, Xi was private secretary to Geng Biao, a senior official who served as Minister of National Defence from 1981 to 1983. Since Xi became party leader, the CCP's concept of national security has changed significantly. It now incorporates the security of all aspects of China's political, social and economic life, including its culture, science and technology, natural resources and nuclear capabilities.

The top intelligence agencies

The various intelligence agencies are under Xi's unified leadership, but they have distinct areas of responsibility. The state, the CCP and the PLA all operate multiple intelligence entities. The reach and significance of these agencies varies, so it is important to understand the functions and leadership of the most powerful of the Chinese intelligence organisations.

The Ministry of State Security sits under the State Council and is tasked with national security and counterintelligence. The current minister is Chen Wenqing. In 2012, after the 18th Party Congress, he became a deputy secretary in the Central Commission for Discipline Inspection, the highest internal control institution of the CCP. Xi has used this commission for an ongoing anti-corruption campaign that has helped to diminish his party rivals and build his faction. In 2015, Chen was appointed party secretary of the Ministry of State Security, and he became its minister in 2016.

Since 2016, the Ministry of State Security has been divided into two core agencies – the National Counterintelligence Agency and the National Intelligence Agency. Modelled on the KGB, the ministry as a whole is organised to target various sensitive groups. Of particular note are its Counterintelligence Division, which spies on foreigners in China; the External Security and Anti-Reconnaissance

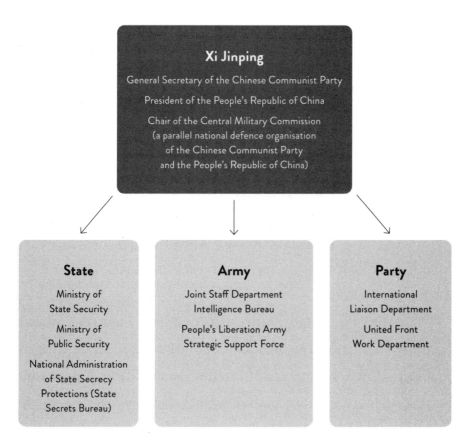

State	Army	Party
Ministry of State Security	Joint Staff Department Intelligence Bureau	International Liaison Department
Ministry of Public Security	People's Liberation Army Strategic Support Force	United Front Work Department
National Administration of State Secrecy Protections (State Secrets Bureau)		

The power of China's intelligence agencies is centralised through Xi Jinping, though the various departments are seeded with both his allies and his enemies.

Division, which monitors Chinese students and scholars abroad; the Social Research Division, which conducts public opinion research in China; the Imaging Intelligence Division, which engages in hacking; and the Enterprises Division, which manages the ministry's front companies. The public face of the ministry is the China Institutes of Contemporary International Relations – the think tank that assessed the PRC as politically weak due to its disastrous handling of

COVID-19. The institute performs open-source research and translation, and its analysts meet with foreign academics and travel abroad as visiting fellows.

Since 2012, the Ministry of Public Security, China's domestic police agency, has also been tasked with national security issues, such as dissent in the Chinese mainland, Hong Kong, Macao and Taiwan, and counterintelligence activities. Guo Shengkun headed the ministry from 2012 to 2017, and the current leader is Zhao Kezhi. Zhao worked for many years with Xi Jinping's close friend Li Zhanshu, who has been on the Politburo Standing Committee since the 19th Party Congress in 2017 and the director of the Office of the National Security Commission since 2014.

Every foreigner who visits China must register with the local Public Security Bureau

The Ministry of Public Security monitors the activities of the foreign population in China. Its vast archives are used for counterintelligence as well as for identifying potential assets. Every foreigner who visits China, whether for a short- or long-term stay, must register with the local Public Security Bureau, which maintains a nationwide database of foreigners' whereabouts in China. Few travellers would understand why their passports and visa status are checked when they register at a hotel. Even Airbnb hosts in China now comply with this requirement. If a foreigner rents an apartment or stays with a foreign or Chinese householder, they must be registered with the bureau within twenty-four hours in an urban area, or within seventy-two hours in a rural area. The Ministry of Public Security also runs the network of surveillance cameras throughout China, which, combined with artificial intelligence, enable a level of supervision of Chinese citizens and foreign residents exceeding that of George Orwell's *Nineteen Eighty-Four*.

The Joint Staff Department Intelligence Bureau of the PLA has been headed by Chen Guangjun since the 19th Party Congress in 2017. Until 2015, this organisation was known as the PLA General Staff Department Intelligence Department, often referred to as the Second Department, or 2PLA. Its name was changed as part of Xi Jinping's shake-up of the PLA leadership and organisational structure. The JSD Intelligence Bureau absorbed the intelligence bureaus of the army, navy, air force and rocket force. It focuses on providing intelligence to support strategic decision-making.

Chen Guangjun has been a beneficiary of Xi's purge of the PLA. From 2009 to 2017, Chen was head of the intelligence bureau of what was then the Second Artillery Force (now the PLA Rocket Force). He is chairman of the China Institute for International Strategic Studies, which is a front organisation of the JSD Intelligence Bureau. The institute co-organises the Xiangshan Forum, the PLA's annual united front event for foreign militaries and security analysts, and issues a weekly intelligence report on foreign military activities.

Since 2015, the PLA's signals intelligence operations have been under the command of a new division of the PLA, known as the Strategic

Support Force. This force reports to the Central Military Commission. Its duties include technical reconnaissance, cyber intelligence, electronic warfare and offensive cyber operations, as well psychological and political warfare. It is led by Gao Jin, who, like Chen Guangjun of the JSD Intelligence Bureau, is one of Xi's "young guard" who benefited from a purge of the PLA senior leadership between 2013 and 2017.

Xi has frequently said that China must prepare for war. The restructuring of the PLA has taken it from being a land-based defensive force to one optimised for warfare. The reorganisation of military intelligence is a crucial part of this. PLA espionage activities have been used in political interference and to help siphon off foreign scientific and economic intelligence to modernise the Chinese military and weaken adversaries. The Strategic Support Force brings these activities together under one agency and reveals the importance the Xi government places on cyber, psychological and political warfare. The PLA had long been the government's primary foreign intelligence provider, as in 1985 the Ministry of State Security had political restrictions placed on its ability to collect information overseas. The restructuring appears to direct PLA intelligence efforts at combat-related activities, while the ministry is now emerging as a full-spectrum intelligence agency. Nonetheless, it will take decades for the ministry to build up the level of intelligence assets and agents the PLA has abroad.

The PLA has been a leading beneficiary of talent-scouting initiatives such as the Thousand Talents Program, which has poured billions of dollars into drawing in tens of thousands of foreign specialists to

China and sends thousands of PRC scientists overseas to access the latest civil- and military-use technology and expertise. In March 2015, the Xi government promoted the merger of civil–military relations in order to expand China's defence sector and improve its technology. The PLA obtains foreign technology by developing international academic links, investing in foreign companies, espionage, hacking and elite capture. It has helped the PLA acquire a variety of innovative technologies such as next-generation fighter jets, advanced missile systems and foundational technologies such as artificial intelligence.

The PLA Institute of International Relations at Nanjing is under the command of the JSD Intelligence Bureau and trains defence attachés and sleeper agents. The PLA has taken advantage of the growth of international education to send its agents abroad via academic exchanges and graduate study, as well as immigration. There are PLA veterans' associations in Australia, Canada, New Zealand and the United Kingdom. A member of the PLA cannot go overseas without official permission, and even after someone retires from active duty they can be restricted from travelling abroad for up to five years. The PLA dispatches undercover agents to work in companies such as China Everbright Group, a state-owned financial conglomerate, and the Bank of China. It also uses its united front "people's diplomacy" organisation, the China Association for International Friendly Contact, as a cover for intelligence work abroad and for asset meetings with foreigners in China. Former PLA personnel often have a prominent role in united front organisations abroad.

PLA military intelligence staff and students who travel abroad commonly disguise the name of their PLA university or employer. New Zealand has a high-profile example of this: National Party MP Jian Yang, a former PLA captain, CCP member, masters graduate and former teacher at the PLA Luoyang Foreign Language Institute, who also studied and taught at the PLA Air Force Engineering University. Both universities train personnel for signals intelligence. Yang gave a false declaration of his background on his application for New Zealand permanent residency, omitting the names of his universities and falsely claiming he had attended Luoyang University. While enrolled in masters and doctoral studies at the Australian National University, Yang founded the Canberra branch of the Chinese Students and Scholars Association, a CCP united front organisation for managing Chinese students, and led it for many years, then later had a high-profile role in united front work activities among overseas Chinese in New Zealand.

A united front against the United Front is quietly forming among like-minded states

Since 2015, the CCP's International Liaison Department (ILD) has been headed by Song Tao, a close associate of Xi. The ILD has more power than the Ministry of Foreign Affairs and has representatives in many of China's embassies. Its influence has greatly increased in the Xi era. The ILD is tasked with gathering intelligence on foreign politicians and political parties, and developing asset relations with them. The ILD's front organisation, the China Association for International Understanding, focuses on co-opting prominent foreign politicians. The ILD nurtures relations with foreign political parties and politicians, offering them access to the CCP leadership for political dialogue, business opportunities and vanity projects in return for public support of China's policies, inside information or, at the very least, silence on critical issues. In 2017, the ILD hosted the World Political Parties Dialogue, attended by representatives from 120 political parties, including the US Republican Party and Japan's Liberal Democratic Party.

The foreign intelligence role of the CCP's United Front Work Department is often overlooked, yet gathering intelligence and running assets are among its main activities. Since the 19th Party Congress in 2017, the department has been headed by Xi associate You Quan. Unlike his immediate predecessors, You is only on the CCP Central Committee, not the Politburo Standing Committee. However, he is secretary of the CCP Secretariat, one of the most influential positions within the party, a role that has traditionally been held by party cadres with a security background.

Xi-era foreign-directed united front activities fall into four key categories: efforts to control the overseas Chinese diaspora and utilise them as agents of Chinese foreign policy; efforts to co-opt foreigners to support and promote the CCP's foreign policy goals; a global, multi-platform communication strategy aimed at promoting China's agenda; and the economic and strategic initiative known as the Belt and Road Initiative. United front work is also important in China's domestic politics, as with the CCP's modernised propaganda activities, the boundaries between national and international united front work are no longer distinct.

The United Front Work Department is the CCP's core foreign subversion organ, and its powers and reach have greatly increased in the Xi era. United front activities are also a task of all CCP party-state-military agencies, as well as a core duty of every CCP member.

In the shadow of Lenin

To understand the connection between united front work and intelligence, it helps to read Lenin. In 1920, Lenin wrote:

> The more powerful enemy can be vanquished only by exerting the utmost effort, and by the most thorough, careful, attentive, skilful and *obligatory* use of any, even the smallest, rift between the enemies, any conflict of interests among the bourgeoisie of the various countries and among the various groups or types of bourgeoisie within the various countries, and also by taking advantage of any, even the smallest, opportunity of winning a mass ally, even though this ally is temporary, vacillating, unstable, unreliable and conditional.

These ideas became part of the core doctrine of CCP underground work – what the party calls united front work. In a 1977 article,

People's Daily approvingly cited the famous quote, concluding, "Those who correctly apply this policy can muster a mighty revolutionary army of the masses in their millions upon millions to concentrate the attack on the chief enemy and triumph in the revolution."

CCP's united front work targets have shifted as its foreign policy has evolved. During World War II, united front efforts were aimed at defeating Japan. During the Chinese Civil War from 1947 to 1949, CCP sleeper agents within the Kuomintang government provided vital intelligence and helped turn the war for the Chinese communists. When the PRC entered the Korean War in 1950, the United States – which the CCP referred to as "the American imperialists" – was promoted as the new government's chief enemy.

From 1961, China was also at odds with the Soviet Union. By the end of the decade, this prompted Mao to seek a temporary alliance with the United States. Thus began the era of the strategic triangle – a classic united front policy – in which the PRC aligned with the United States and its partners against the Soviet Union. The quasi-alliance was formalised in meetings between US secretary of state Henry Kissinger and the CCP leadership from 1969 to 1972.

The end of the Cold War and the collapse of the Soviet Union in 1991 removed the justification for the strategic triangle, as Kissinger admitted in his 2011 book *On China*. In internal speeches in 1989 to both CCP personnel and foreign leaders, PRC leader Deng Xiaoping depicted the April–June 1989 student protest movement as a US-inspired effort to bring down the CCP. From the perspective of successive CCP leaders, the United States has continually engaged in subversion and division, by supporting democracy activities within China, through its espionage activities and by providing military support to Taiwan.

In the Xi era, the United States is once again China's chief enemy and the main target of espionage and other covert activities. The PRC targets US partners and allies such as Australia, Canada, New Zealand, the United Kingdom and the other NATO states in order to fracture US alliances and weaken the power of its main opponent.

Few international intelligence agencies have many Chinese-speaking specialists

How to counter CCP espionage and interference

In our current era of great-power competition and hybrid warfare, raw military strength may no longer be as significant to the security of small and medium powers such as Australia, Canada and New Zealand as strong cyber-defence capabilities, national resilience and unity. Many foreign governments are now facing up to the impact of covert CCP activities on the integrity of their political systems, and making a correction in their relationship with China.

Governments should engage with China on trade where it is possible to do so constructively, but must avoid trade dependency. They should set sensible boundaries in the relationship and pass new laws to address the CCP's espionage and political interference activities. A united front against the United Front is quietly forming among like-minded states, with new agreements between countries on supply chains, and partnerships on technology policies such as 5G and the supply of strategic materials.

Many governments are in the process of investigating covert CCP activity in their countries and adopting plans to counteract it. Some have released findings publicly. Australia and New Zealand have updated legislation on matters such as electoral financing, protocols around conflicts of interest for past and former members of central and local governments, and foreign sales of strategic infrastructure and land. The next big challenge is for these governments to establish a genuine and positive relationship with their ethnic Chinese populations and support them to become resilient and autonomous from CCP attempts to control them and utilise them in espionage.

National security is a concern for every citizen. Our political leaders must be confident to speak frankly about the risks, as well as the opportunities, of relations with the party-state-military-market nexus. An informed society is crucial. More public information about CCP espionage and political interference will help individuals, political leaders and government agencies to make better choices on China-related activities. For example, politicians and governments should distinguish between genuine ethnic community activities and proxies for united front work.

The foreign targets of CCP espionage and political interference must make a long-term investment in capacities to help deal with the challenges China under Xi Jinping poses. In 2017, Xi made himself "president for life", and his control over China's intelligence agencies gives him more power than any leader since Mao Zedong. Few international intelligence agencies have many Chinese-speaking specialists, let alone ones with an in-depth understanding of the party-state-military-market nexus. Knowledge of Chinese intelligence agencies should be a standard feature of the workplace education of politicians, diplomats and other public servants. People in these roles, as well as the public, should be informed about Ministry of State Security, commonly known as the MSS, and other CCP spy agencies, whose acronyms – and key activities – should be just as familiar to us as those of the CIA or the KGB. ∎

THE END OF ORTHODOXY

Australia in a
post-pandemic world

Penny Wong

Before COVID-19, the world was already experiencing heightened disruption. Brexit, the election of Donald Trump, China's growing assertiveness, rising nationalism and the increasingly competitive relationship between the world's two great powers had dramatically destabilised the global order.

Then came the novel coronavirus pandemic. This is a new scale of disruption that could further unravel or even destroy the rules-based system we have known since World War II. There has been a shocking loss of life, with more to come. Statistics and graphs go some way to capturing the devastation, but the images of overwhelmed hospitals, mass graves and fearful communities speak universally and power- fully. It is a shared experience of grief.

The breadth of economic harm is almost unprecedented. The International Monetary Fund (IMF) predicts the worst global recession since the Great Depression. The IMF has made an extraordinary shift from its pre-COVID expectations of positive per-capita income growth in 160 nations to predict negative growth in 170. A surge of financial crises across the globe has already begun.

We do not yet have a sense of the full extent of the damage the pandemic may wreak in the developing world. But the vulnerability of the world's poorest people is patent – they will suffer more fatalities, increased poverty and greater instability. The United Nations World Food Programme is warning of an unprecedented hunger emergency, with "multiple famines of biblical proportions". Over 265 million people will face acute hunger by the end of this year.

Our capacity to respond is affected not only by the weaker economic positions of the G20 nations and shakier balance sheets among corporates, banks and households going into the crisis, but also by a lack of global coordination.

This is the stark truth that we must confront. In the midst of the worst crisis humanity has experienced since World War II and a severe economic downturn of unknown proportions, the international community has been unable to muster anything close to the requisite cooperation. Nations have been too mired in mistrust to generate a sense of common purpose. Competition and disinformation abound. Unlike in the global financial crisis (GFC) of 2007–08, this catastrophe appears to have reinforced a macho strain of nationalism, and confrontation rather than cooperation. The cost of this collective failure will be measured in deaths and suffering.

COVID-19 will reshape our lives, our country, the global economy and the world. How much and for how long is unclear. Policymakers cannot afford to be passive. Our economic and public health responses couldn't wait for perfect information; they had to recognise the imperative to act and the grim consequences of inaction.

We now need to bring a similar sense of urgency and purpose to Australian foreign policy. This will involve assessing the post-pandemic challenges honestly, articulating them clearly and harnessing our collective resources to tackle them effectively. Our success in suppressing the virus at home is only the beginning, and as the world re-forms in the wake of this crisis, we will need to adapt quickly.

Australia's response must begin by examining some key questions. What does this pandemic mean for the global power balance? What does it mean for multilateralism and our region's stability? How should we prepare for the increasing international disorder? In short, how do we protect and promote our national interests in the COVID-19 era?

Richard Haass, president of the Council on Foreign Relations, observes that COVID-19 has brought into "sharper-than-ever relief" the characteristics of the pre-pandemic world: "waning American leadership, faltering global cooperation, great-power discord". For Australia, these trends comprise fundamental challenges. Our strategic environment has deteriorated, risks have heightened, opportunities narrowed, and protecting and promoting our national interests is going to be much harder.

Intensifying great-power competition

The most significant of these trends is the increasingly divergent paths taken by the United States and China. Both are challenging the status quo in different ways, and each views the other as a strategic competitor. Before COVID-19, this competition was increasingly defining their intent and driving their behaviour. The pandemic is intensifying this dynamic. Bonnie S. Glaser, senior advisor for Asia at the Center for Strategic and International Studies, summarises bluntly: "The rivalry, which even before the virus extended to all aspects of the relationship – economic, military, diplomatic and ideological – will accelerate the decoupling of the two economies and deepen mistrust between the countries and their peoples."

The pandemic has brought nationalism to the fore, along with xenophobia

The United States is right to point to China's lack of transparency in the early days of the pandemic. China's suppression of information and warnings about the virus are well documented. There are also reports, including from London's *The Times* in March 2020, about the ordered destruction of virus samples, compromising studies to inform the public health response.

China has hardened its campaign to promote its success in controlling the outbreak. But it has gone further, including by allowing its diplomats to falsely claim that the US Army brought the virus to China. US Secretary of State Mike Pompeo has backed claims the virus was created in a Chinese laboratory – an allegation repeated by an Australian minister despite being discounted by the US and Australian intelligence communities.

President Trump, meanwhile, has referred to the "Chinese virus" and has announced the United States will terminate its relationship with the World Health Organization, describing it as "China-centric". US insistence on a reference to the "Wuhan virus" resulted in the scrapping of a joint communiqué after the G7 Foreign Ministers' Meeting (held by video conference) on 27 March 2020.

As the contest of narratives between the United States and China intensifies, their competitive behaviour has also escalated, with our region a focal point. China's recent unilateral actions in the South China Sea have included the sinking of a Vietnamese fishing vessel in the vicinity of the Paracel Islands, establishing "administrative districts" on the Paracel and Spratly Islands, and warning that any attempt to deny its claims of sovereignty in the South China Sea will be doomed to fail.

There is little evidence that US–China competition will abate. Both nations' assessments of their interests and identities are deepening the rivalry. Both disregard the practical limits of this com-petition – that neither can contain or fully exclude the other. Nor is there any obvious attempt to identify a settling point – a desired end state of their competition that would provide clarity to our region, particularly as countries grapple with increasingly fractured supply chains that span the globe and depend on reliable market access.

It is not in Australia's interests to concentrate solely on this binary of US–China competition. As a US ally, security partner and friend, we have already made a choice. But that is not the end of the matter.

Nationalism rising, multilateralism fracturing

The pandemic has brought nationalism to the fore, along with its occasional companions xenophobia, nativism and isolationism. This has contributed to the absence of a coordinated international response to the crisis and, left unbridled, risks compromising the path to recovery.

The respective brands of nationalism in the United States and China are driving their distrust and unravelling the rules-based order, both institutionally and normatively. US global leadership has given way to an American nationalism, crisply summarised as "America First". At the same time, a more strident Chinese nationalism has become a feature of President Xi's leadership – both at home and abroad. As researcher at the Australian Strategic Policy Institute Vicky Xiuzhong Xu argues, Chinese nationalism today is "centered on the narrative that China has been a victim of colonization and the current world order, and that the Communist Party is the only savior".

Notwithstanding its unmatched global power, America's role in the world has changed. Prior to the pandemic, the United States had already withdrawn from UNESCO, the UN Human Rights Council, the Paris Climate Agreement and the Trans-Pacific Partnership, and engaged in a "war of attrition" with the World

Trade Organization by blocking nominees to the Appellate Body. The withdrawal from the WHO in the midst of a global pandemic is the most recent display of the administration's rejection of the multilateral system.

There's no doubt the multilateral system is in need of reform. Aspects of the WTO's structures, rules and standards do not suit today's world – an example of a consensus-based approach leading to paralysis. And perceptions of political interference have hampered the WHO's clarity of message in responding to the COVID-19 pandemic. But those institutions are a function of the states that fund, shape and resource them – vacating the space is rarely a successful reform strategy.

Meanwhile, China is increasing its influence in and support of the multilateral system, consistent with President Xi's express articulation in 2017 that "reforming and developing the global governance system" is a major foreign policy priority. China's growing assertiveness is prompting uncertainty about its ambitions, including whether it seeks pre-eminent global leadership, and whether it wants a more illiberal form of global governance designed to suit the interests of authoritarian states.

Collective responses to common threats benefit all nations, great and small. We saw this most recently in the cooperation that enabled our recovery from the GFC. Yet today, facing greater economic devastation, as well as loss of life and global health risks, the pandemic is leading to increased fragmentation. The UN Security Council could not agree that COVID-19 was a threat to international peace and security, while the G20, the engine room of our response to the GFC, has been unable to rally a coordinated economic response.

In part, this is because the United States, China and members of the European Union have grappled with domestic outbreaks of the virus. There hasn't been much bandwidth for focus beyond the homeland. But this is a lost opportunity – as research by Brookings has shown, fiscal stimulus gives a bigger boost to economies when it is coordinated across countries. Cooperation prevents beggar-thy-neighbour policies and can help stop financial crises in emerging and developing economies. The longer we let international challenges fester, the harder and more costly they will be to address.

Collective responses to common threats benefit all nations, great and small

The liberal rules-based order is increasingly fragile in the COVID-19 era. Its institutions have been weakened. Its philosophical bases – including the principle that collective challenges need collective solutions – have been undermined. And, in the absence of a great-power champion, it will continue to suffer from a lack of stability.

In this, Australia's national interests differ substantively from those of the United States and China. John McCarthy, a former ambassador and high commissioner to the United States, Indonesia and India, reminds us that "small and medium powers need rules more than big ones". We need the multilateral system to set the rules by which we trade, invest, travel, enforce international boundaries, mediate conflicts, uphold human rights, deliver vital services – including healthcare – to those most in need, and address climate change. Effective multilateralism ameliorates the raw power politics of the bigger players and enables us to have a say in building collective solutions to global problems. For Australia, policy and diplomatic leadership to reform the multilateral system is a key national interest.

Resilience, not isolationism

The global trend towards nationalism also presents risks for economic recovery from the COVID-19 crisis. While international trade grew at twice the rate of gross domestic product for half a century, the pandemic is exacerbating a retreat from globalisation. It has led to calls for greater economic self-reliance, restructuring of supply chains and, more broadly, the unwinding of economic integration. For those in the United States who have argued for a "decoupling", the pandemic is "proof" of the imperative.

Undeniably, the pandemic has exposed the risks of the globalised system. For instance, the mobility of people propelled the virus across the planet, forcing a near-complete halt to international travel and casting doubt over the long-term viability of aviation and tourism as we know them. Supply chains that prioritised efficiency left critical sectors vulnerable.

It is reasonable for Australia to focus on enhancing the nation's resilience to external shocks, including how to safeguard critical sectors and industries. But we cannot allow a descent into populism – or worse, xenophobia – and we must resist calls for autarky. Isolationism and the fragmentation of the global economy will delay recovery for Australia and the world. Trade has substantially reduced the cost of living for Australians and has made us more innovative, competitive and productive. Economic engagement with the world has increased national income and created Australian jobs. Exports now contribute more than $400 billion to the Australian economy, or 24 per cent of GDP, and one in five jobs. Over 70 per cent of Australia's agricultural production is exported. More than 25 per cent of our tourism industry relies on international visitors, to say nothing of the contribution of universities and mining. A path to recovery in which trade is not a crucial component is inconceivable.

Neither the unbridled free market nor economic isolationism will enhance Australia's resilience to future disruptions – the right policies lie in between.

The pandemic has led to an intensifying debate about the extent of Australia's economic engagement with China. This discussion should be conducted sensibly and soberly, and should not be dismissive of China's economic weight and the depth of our economic ties.

It is in both nations' interests to maintain a productive relationship as we emerge from this crisis. This relationship will become more difficult to navigate, but disengagement is not an option. Instead, we need fewer partisan pronouncements and a closer focus on the terms of our engagement. For example, there is merit in more practical guidance in certain sectors, including research and education, so that organisations are better equipped to manage risks and complexities. There must also be more dialogue with the Australian people on the benefits and challenges of our ties with China. We need to move beyond sweeping generalisations to a considered understanding of how to make the relationship work for us, including managing our differences.

Building the region we want

As we grapple with the pandemic at home, amid an anaemic global response, we cannot lose sight of its impact on our immediate region. In navigating the effects of both the pandemic and great-power competition, Australian foreign policy should remain guided by the kind of region we want: a region in which outcomes are not determined only by power, and in which there is shared support for international rules and norms to guide behaviour and enable collective action to resolve disputes.

Rory Medcalf, head of the National Security College at the Australian National University, argues that the Indo-Pacific region is too large and too diverse for one country to dominate. But it is becoming more contested, and Australia will need to work to maintain an equilibrium that enables a multipolar region with the attributes we seek and that prevents hegemony. This requires developing deep partnerships, particularly with Indonesia, India, Japan, Korea and Singapore, as well as through the Association of Southeast Asian Nations (ASEAN) and the Pacific Islands Forum (PIF).

Yet the pandemic's economic impacts on key partners in the region may hinder this plan. South-East Asia is highly vulnerable to a financial crisis as its states face unprecedented financial pressure. Emerging economies around the world are grappling with capital outflows – at multiples of those seen in the GFC – and spiralling debt costs through a potent combination of collapsing exchange rates, loss of export income and rising bond yields. These vulnerabilities are particularly acute in Indonesia, a country that is central to containing financial contagion in the region. Jakarta's substantial economic and financial reforms could not have prepared it for this one-in-a-hundred-year shock. And Indonesian policymakers haven't forgotten the impacts – positive and negative – of the IMF's response during the country's last financial shock in 1997. Australia and the region cannot afford for Indonesia to founder, and we must stand ready to assist it.

We can help galvanise a multilateral response for the region

Australia's stability and prosperity rely on a stable and prosperous South-East Asia. The nations that comprise ASEAN, and ASEAN as an entity, are crucial to maintaining regional security. But few ASEAN member-states have the resources to deal comprehensively with the health and economic effects of the pandemic. There is a risk that COVID-19 could lead to multiple crises – humanitarian, economic and internal security – with serious ramifications for the wider stability of the region. India, too, faces the pandemic with vulnerabilities, including slowing growth, a weak financial system, widespread poverty and inadequate health and social security safety nets.

To avert this crisis is challenging. As Roland Rajah, director of the International Economics Program at the Lowy Institute, points out, both Indonesia and India are too large for Australia to play a "decisive role". But our contribution should include health assistance and enhanced financial support – including existing Reserve Bank currency swap arrangements with our partners most exposed to financial shocks. Most importantly, we can harness our political and intellectual capital to help galvanise a multilateral response for the region. Australia has substantial capacity to do this, as demonstrated by our role in the G20's successful management of the GFC, and by our leading public health capabilities.

We know that further pandemics will emerge. Drawing on the successful model of the Jakarta Centre for Law Enforcement Cooperation, developed in response to the terrorism threat, Australia could partner with both South-East Asia and the South Pacific, through ASEAN and the PIF, on a regional pandemic prevention initiative, looking at sanitation, live animal markets and the interactions between animals and humans.

The pandemic will also have major implications for the Pacific.

Fragile health systems could be overwhelmed, and those Pacific countries that most depend on tourism face virtual economic collapse. A clear strategy to provide assistance, in concert with Pacific partners and like-minded donors, will be critical. This assistance should be targeted at boosting healthcare resources as well as lobbying for speedy action from international financial institutions to assist Pacific economic recovery. Any perception that Australia has let its Pacific partners down at this time of need or is not listening to them could fundamentally compromise the Pacific "step-up" policy.

We will also need continued and constructive US engagement in the Indo-Pacific. This is a prerequisite of the multipolar region we seek. It may prove challenging as America grapples with its own crises. Our nations' differing views on strengthening the multilateral system and the retreat of US global leadership will make the effort more complicated still. Nevertheless, we will need to find a way to manage these differences with our ally, even as doing so becomes more difficult.

Reimagining our foreign policy

The pandemic has made the world a riskier place. Responding to these risks is demanding, especially when we face economic and health challenges at home. But if we do not act now, it will only become harder to manage these risks in the future.

First, we need to find the capacity to focus on these external challenges: to assess them honestly, to articulate them and to harness our collective resources to address them. Our national security demands it. Australia is not a mere bystander in the world, and certainly not in Asia. What Australia says and does matters. We have the capacity to actively shape the region's future and Australia's place in it – alongside our partners in the region.

Second, we must be prepared to invest financially and intellectually in the stability of our region. Our shared interest in mitigating humanitarian and financial crises means Australia needs to significantly and visibly increase our outreach and presence, particularly in South-East Asia and the Pacific. We need to invest in the building blocks of these partnerships, including development assistance, diplomatic resources and economic ties. A Pacific step-up that is accompanied by a South-East Asian step down is an own goal. We will need to be ready to help bolster Indonesia's response – as our largest and closest neighbour, its economic recovery is tied to ours. We should help strengthen regional-level responses through ASEAN and the PIF and help galvanise a multilateral response through international financial institutions. The pandemic is amplifying pre-existing inequalities, so our response must address the economic, political and social disparities faced by women and girls, particularly in our region.

We need to continue to broaden our engagement with India, including through the implementation of Peter Varghese's India Economic Strategy, prepared for the Department of Foreign Affairs, and drawing on links enabled by the Indian diaspora here in Australia.

The Strategy – which has been gathering dust for two years – rightly identifies our education sector, together with our agriculture, resources and tourism credentials, as the frontrunners of cooperation and growth. India is central to a regional equilibrium and shares our interest in achieving it – but we should remain realistic about its economic and social challenges.

Importantly, that sense of partnership and shared purpose with others in the region needs to be integrated into our thinking, our language, our engagement. We want the nations of ASEAN and the Pacific to be secure and prosperous because their security and prosperity are ours, too. Former prime minister Paul Keating rightly said that Australia needed to seek its security in Asia, not from Asia. Australia's influence is enhanced when we move from "them" to "us".

Australia needs to be more self-reliant in protecting and promoting our interests

Third, we need to renew the multilateral system. Australia has a long history of making international institutions more effective and equitable. We need to reprise that enthusiasm for reform – starting with a more strategic approach to supporting key candidacies and a more active promotion of Australian expertise within these institutions.

The world now needs an articulation of principles for a multilateralism that works for the post-COVID era and for the global challenges that lie ahead – including maintaining an open, rules-based trading system, resisting protectionism, upholding and strengthening the UN Convention on the Law of the Sea, and ensuring strong and effective development and financial institutions. The Atlantic Charter – drafted during the peak global disruption of World War II – reminds us of a time when great powers articulated such principles. Today, we need others to step forward. Australia can and should be at the forefront of crafting the operating principles of the post-COVID world.

Contrary to the nationalist rhetoric from some politicians, multilateralism hasn't diminished our sovereignty. Instead, it is one of Australia's most effective tools in managing global risks. It can contribute to the region we want. It is also a prerequisite for a comprehensive global response to climate change, in which Australia has a deep national interest. Climate change is the next pandemic.

We need to work around the roadblocks generated by great-power competition. The best hedge for Australia is more active cooperation with other substantial powers. While this obviously means we need to better utilise existing architecture, including the East Asia Summit and the Asia-Pacific Economic Cooperation, the future will also require Australian foreign policy to go beyond what we have known – to risk articulating different approaches. We must have the confidence and will to shape the outcomes we seek, rather than being caught in the slipstream of the strategic competition between the United States and China.

We should cultivate new, informal associations of countries with common interests, forming compacts on pressing issues where global consensus is elusive. By building shared foundations – on issues as diverse as maritime security, clean energy, trade, infrastructure, health and governance – Australia can also strengthen its status as a regional leader and partner of choice.

Moreover, we need to be sober about the impacts of the deteriorating US–China relationship. Australia will need to work harder to manage the risks and consequences of escalation, as their mutual distrust shows no sign of abatement. This places a greater premium on self-reliance and the preparedness to assert our interests.

Our relationship with China, as with any other country, must be guided by our values and interests – including transparency and sovereignty. However, the escalation of anti-China rhetoric or anti-Chinese sentiment for domestic electoral purposes benefits neither our society nor our standing in the world.

These tasks – renewing the multilateral system, deepening partnerships in South-East Asia and the Pacific, and navigating a more volatile US–China relationship – are not simple. All require a more active foreign policy and a deeper investment in our diplomacy – and the recognition that Australia needs to be more self-reliant in protecting and promoting our interests.

The necessity for greater self-reliance imposes corresponding disciplines on our politics. Nationalism, xenophobia and even extremism are on the rise. There are some things which must be beyond politics, and our collective response to these should demonstrate that. We must always recall the lessons of the 1930s. Humanity has seen what happens if we allow nationalism and xenophobia to take hold.

This crisis will demand the maturity to set aside domestic partisanship. Public interventions and rhetorical grenades designed to gain attention or tactical advantage serve little purpose, and distract from the far more challenging task at hand. Put simply, we don't have time for "negative globalism". We need to think about thirty-year horizons, not three-year election cycles.

The global disruption in recent years has already generated sharp domestic debate about foreign policy. It will be even more difficult to confront change of the magnitude we now face. It can generate resistance and denial.

Our external circumstances since the end of World War II have been comparatively benign. This has been a period characterised by stability and growth, in which our principal security partner was the dominant global power, and the multilateral system largely served our interests well. But much has changed. COVID-19 will intensify this. Navigating this world will require not only sound judgment and creativity – it will also demand a new foreign policy ambition. It will require us to accept and fully exercise our agency. It will require consistency and discipline.

Most of all, it will require leadership. ▪

THE FIX

Solving Australia's foreign affairs challenges

—

Susan Harris Rimmer on How Australia Can Shape the G20 Agenda

"Australia has made an impact on the G20 recently, showing that our leadership is welcomed ... It could do more with the right support."

THE PROBLEM: The Group of Twenty (G20) is an association of twenty advanced economies whose purpose is to promote "strong, sustainable, balanced and inclusive growth". It has been meeting at the ministerial level since 1999 and the leader level since 2008. Australia is a member, along with other major economies such as China, Germany, India, Indonesia, Japan, the United Kingdom, the United States and the European Union.

The G20 is increasingly important to the management of the global economy. It played a major role in bringing back financial stability during the 2007–08 global financial crisis

(GFC), including committing to a US$5 trillion stimulus in April 2009. Research by Brookings has shown that the impact of fiscal stimulus can double when it is coordinated across the G20. One of Australia's previous sherpas, or personal representatives of the government, David Gruen, has said the measures the G20 implemented during the GFC directly and indirectly affected Australian lives.

Between crises, the G20 has tried to encourage cooperation between the established powers of the G7 and the emerging powers of China, India and others, especially through measures to combat protectionism. This has been crucial to Australia's interests as an open economy. Right now, the G20 needs to step up again. COVID-19 is a health crisis that is also an exogenous shock to the global economy, hitting supply and demand simultaneously. The G20 leaders met virtually in March and pledged to inject US$5 trillion in fiscal spending into the global economy and to "do whatever it takes to overcome the pandemic". They will need to build confidence that the crisis is being effectively tackled inside and across borders or the economic uncertainty will increase.

There are a range of policy areas in which Australia, through its membership of the G20, could play a more active role. These include the economic impacts of disasters such as bushfires and pandemics, the future of the digital economy, the importance of rule-based trade, and investment in regional infrastructure.

But Australia is not doing enough to use its G20 membership to try to influence the international agenda.

Part of the problem is that there is little public engagement or scrutiny, as it is not easy for Australians to follow the G20's activities. Member states, including Australia, have deliberately not set up a secretariat or administrative support unit, hoping to maintain more flexibility. When Australia hosted the G20 in Brisbane in 2014, there was an associated website with resources, now archived. From 2012 to 2016 the government invested in a G20 Studies Centre at the Lowy Institute, which provided pivotal analysis; its website is also now archived. The G20 page on the Department of Foreign Affairs and Trade website sends readers to a Canadian university resource hub. The only other source of public information is the Twitter account, which chronicles the activities of Australia's current sherpa, Simon Duggan. Clearly, Australia's inertia on providing information about the G20 is hindering both transparency and our incentive to influence.

THE PROPOSAL: Australia should create a G20 institute to develop policy and maximise our influence. This institute could sit within a government ministry or at a university or think tank, or be established as an independent entity, like the Global Infrastructure Hub, set up by the G20 in Sydney to support policymaking for global infrastructure projects.

The institute would mix retired Australian officials with deep knowledge of G20 processes, such as former G20 sherpa Gordon de Brouwer and former G20 finance deputy Mike Callaghan, with government, academic, business and community stakeholders. It could produce timely research as well as inclusive events.

The G20 institute's mission would be to:

- allow public access to information about what Australia is doing at the G20
- drive global economic policy change
- secure Australia's key objectives from each summit
- help facilitate deeper economic engagement with the Asia-Pacific, particularly with fellow G20 members China, Japan, South Korea, Indonesia and India.

Before each G20 summit, the institute would analyse the Australian government's policy objectives. After each summit, it would assess implementation of these objectives, and the potential for action in other forums, such as the Asia-Pacific Economic Cooperation (APEC), the Association of Southeast Asian Nations (ASEAN) and the United Nations. It would also encourage critical conversations about how the G20 can best function.

The institute would foster international collaboration and actively promote and communicate the results of this work. It would do so widely, including to policymakers and academics as well as to the business and non-governmental sectors. This could involve publishing policy papers, hosting conferences, establishing a student ambassador program, encouraging academic and student exchanges and engaging in community outreach.

Finally, the institute would be a G20 resource centre, collecting and providing access to papers, documents, statements and other materials created to pursue the G20's global mission. It would support the activities and meetings of the growing list of stakeholder groups, such as the B20, which represents business leaders from the G20 members; the L20, which represents the global trade union movement; the W20, which represents women's organisations and female entrepreneurs; and the Young Entrepreneurs' Alliance.

Former federal treasurer Wayne Swan created the G20 Studies Centre at the Lowy Institute with a A$4 million grant from Treasury. Today, the need for such an institute is growing as the G20's agenda is becoming more complex. Many expect that it will respond to shortcomings in the US- and European-dominated Bretton Woods system (the International Monetary Fund, the World Bank and the World Trade Organization), and the participation of stakeholder groups is adding a new dimension to its engagement with civil society.

WHY IT WILL WORK: The G20 should not be a focus of government investment only when Australia is the host. It is not a sporting event or other tourism driver.

The forum is important to Australia's national interest, and our membership is not guaranteed, as there is no formal qualification process. The Department of Foreign Affairs and Trade notes that "Australia benefits from G20 cooperation to support an open global economy and to protect the global financial system's stability". Australia needs to ensure that future G20 summits keep faith with the government's foreign and international economic policy positions.

The G20 has driven reforms to the international tax system to stop corporate tax evasion, through the OECD G20 Base Erosion and Profit Shifting Project and the promotion of tax transparency standards. Australia has implemented these reforms with domestic legislation. The G20 has also committed to reduce the gap between male and female workforce participation by 25 per cent by 2025, which would add more than 100 million women to the global labour force. This goal was translated to the Australian strategy "Towards 2025", which aims for more affordable, accessible and flexible childcare, and greater support for female entrepreneurs.

Australia has made an impact on the G20 recently, showing that our leadership is welcomed. In June 2019, Prime Minister Scott Morrison brokered a declaration at the G20 summit in

Osaka, Japan, to put new pressure on Facebook and other social media giants to halt the spread of violent terrorism online in the wake of the Christchurch attacks. Morrison was one of nine leaders who scored an invite to the Outreach Session in the lead-up to the G7 Summit in France in August 2019. At the meeting, Australia worked with the OECD to fund the development of voluntary reporting protocols for social media companies to prevent, detect and remove terrorist and violent extremist content. It could do more with the right support.

When then foreign minister Julie Bishop commissioned the 2017 Foreign Policy White Paper in December 2016, she noted it was designed to help Australian diplomacy be more proactive. She said the aim was to ensure "that we're not reacting to events, we're strategically positioned to manage, maybe even shape, events". In order to shape the G20, Australia needs to do more than just turn up. It needs to leverage its membership, so it can play an active role in promoting international cooperation and steering the global economy.

THE RESPONSE: DFAT would not say whether the government supported the creation of a permanent G20 institute. However, a spokesperson for the department said Australia "supports a strong and effective G20 as the premier forum for international economic cooperation". "This cooperation is particularly important now as the world faces unprecedented economic, health and social challenges," the spokesperson said. "Australia will continue to leverage the G20 to proactively advocate for our interests and protect the foundations of economic success, open markets and the rules-based trading system."

Dedicated to the memory of Russell Trood

Reviews

Contest for the Indo-Pacific: Why China Won't Map the Future
Rory Medcalf
Black Inc.

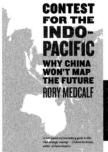

After a year of uncertainty about how the new US administration was going to approach Asia, in late 2017 President Trump set out his vision at the APEC CEO summit in Da Nang, Vietnam. There he declared that the United States would champion a "free and open Indo-Pacific". The speech marked the adoption of the term "Indo-Pacific" – which was mentioned ten times – as the formal description of the region by its most powerful state. Think-tankers had argued for it since 2012,

and countries such as Australia and Japan had previously deployed it in their foreign and defence policy pronouncements. But when Washington moved on from the rhetoric of the "Asia-Pacific", the battle of ideas seemed to have been won.

Rory Medcalf, of the Australian National University's National Security College, was an early adopter and is a long-time spruiker of the Indo-Pacific construct. In this intriguing book, he sets out to explain a label that has not captured the public's imagination to the same degree as it has policymakers'. He also seeks to describe the region's current competitiveness, and to articulate what he believes to be the best way to manage China, by his reckoning the most disruptive force in the region.

The notion of the Indo-Pacific describes a widening geographic expanse of connectivity as states, societies and security interests in the Asia-Pacific and the Indian Ocean regions are bound by growing economic ties. But, as Medcalf makes clear, it also serves a larger purpose: organising a collective response to China "without resorting to capitulation or conflict".

The book has real strengths.

It shows convincingly that Asia's future will not be determined by the nature of Sino–American relations alone. The eponymous contest involves multiple countries, both great and small, jostling for influence. Also, Medcalf correctly emphasises that lesser powers have a role to play in shaping the dynamics of competition and the possibilities for cooperation. Australia, Japan, Vietnam and the Philippines, to name but four, are not helplessly bobbing in an ocean of great-power rivalry. While his high-speed jog through the past to explain how we got to the Indo-Pacific offers little new, other than some unconvincing attempts to paint the Indo-Pacific as a zone of activity that has always been with us, his argument for how to manage China is original and should be taken seriously.

Medcalf contends that countries which do not want to live in a region dominated by China must undertake a coordinated pushback – an approach that carries the risk of significant human and economic costs. It will require Australia and others to pay a good deal more – from higher taxes or foregone government services – as we sharpen our swords against a vital trading partner.

It may even mean some have to die.

Yet Medcalf is to be applauded for calling on governments to improve their engagement with the public about strategic policy and its inherent costs and risks. Australia has already committed to significantly enhance its capacity to fight wars. It is vital that we talk openly and honestly about this, and the trade-offs we will have to make if we advance his vision.

However, as a book that is supposed to make the case for the importance of the Indo-Pacific label, it is curiously ineffective. The public are not going to stop referring to Asia in favour of "the Indo-Pacific" any time soon. Indeed, in some respects that part of the book is redundant; the label is not really what matters. Where the notion of the Indo-Pacific makes its contribution is as a device to organise policy in a contested geopolitical climate. It is, despite protestations from the author and others, all about China. This reality sits oddly with the book's occasional complaint about China taking issue with the term.

The author's assessment of China is also somewhat curious. He takes a very critical stance on the party-state – with good reason, given the horrors of Xinjiang and elsewhere. The country is characterised as menacing and strategically malign, but also foolish and almost naive. It is a country that does not understand the eternal verities of the Indo-Pacific and often, in his view, misunderstands key regional developments.

The characterisation of China's Belt and Road Initiative (BRI) exemplifies this. In Medcalf's telling, the BRI is a strategic vision of an alternate regional order where China dominates both sea and land. But, he believes, it is also a deeply flawed project, a form of neo-colonialism that will alienate more than it attracts, and whose scale will drive China to imperial overstretch and increase the possibility of military conflict.

Ultimately, the book argues that engagement with China is neither possible nor wise. It is a power one cannot trust, whose "military has a grip on foreign policy, reminiscent at times of the hardline officer class in 1930s Tokyo". Consequently, it is a country with which one must coexist and, when imposed upon, resist. There is no consideration that China may change. Just as ten years ago few

thought China's future would be a neo-Maoist techno-surveillance state, it would be equally wrong to think that the People's Republic of China will remain forever as it is. Certainly it is hard to imagine a shift from the current trajectory under Xi Jinping. But as Harvard strategist William Overholt has argued, Xi's concentration of offices and cult of personality is a function of his weakness, not his strength. One day he will be gone, and quite possibly much sooner than many think.

Closing the door to any kind of cooperation, and planning only coexistence and pushback, will make it more likely that even if Xi were to be toppled by Chinese Communist Party grandees, the country would already have been pressed into a corner.

The shadow of COVID-19 looms over the book's central arguments. For Medcalf, China is weaker than many assume, and the United States stronger and more durable. Yet once the world is through the virus, there is a good chance that Beijing's hand will be strengthened and Washington's weakened. The economic consequences of the pandemic are likely to echo for years and will be another front in Sino–American rivalry.

Over the past decade, Asia has become increasingly integrated and contested. Medcalf presents a highly readable account of its past and a prescription for shaping its future. But his vision mistakes a key aspect: the future will be China-centred but not Sino-centric. As such, the argument to bypass engagement and focus on resisting Chinese influence is ultimately mistaken.

Even as the region is organised increasingly around Beijing, no state, including the PRC, will be able to have things entirely their own way. Other Asian powers can and must work together to bind China into the system and to cajole, socialise and, when needed, coerce it when it steps out of line. China has to have a seat at the regional table. To focus only on pushback is to ensure the region's future is highly militarised, which would make us all worse off.

Nick Bisley

**The Dragons
and the Snakes:
How the Rest Learned
to Fight the West**
David Kilcullen
Scribe Publications

A favoured line of David Kilcullen's, which I've shamelessly recycled, is that economists deal with pessimism while strategists deal in cataclysm. Kilcullen is a highly appropriate sherpa for these cataclysmic times. Pandemic has seemingly turned globalisation on its head, economic power is being rapidly disrupted, strategic faultlines are on display and "the West" is in paroxysms of self-doubt and grief over a slipping geopolitical order.

The importance of Kilcullen's work to Western military thought is clear. There would be very few Australian Army officers serving this century who haven't had their thinking informed and more likely shaped by Kilcullen's insights. As a scholar-practitioner, he has fluently translated military art and science for public debate, particularly through his writing on Afghanistan, Iraq and Islamic State. He can both stalk the halls of power and understand what happens when bullet meets flesh.

In this book, he chooses 1993 as the marker of a shift, in Western militaries, from post–Cold War technical triumph to a quarter-century of malaise. Specifically, he adopts the evocative testimony of President Clinton's CIA director James Woolsey, who categorises threats to the West into dragons (state-based threats) and snakes (everything else) and warns that the snakes may be harder to track. Dragons and snakes makes for a catchy title, but as an analytical framework it is at times more burden than bedrock, distracting from the weightier insights this book delivers.

Kilcullen begins by considering aspects of Western warfare that state and non-state actors have had to commonly adapt to in the past twenty-five years, and proposes a theory, informed by biology and complex systems thinking, of how the West has in fact driven that evolution. In this, Kilcullen is on strong ground. He has spent decades examining the "combat Darwinism" of insurgent groups in the Middle East, seeking to rapidly translate tactical battlefield data from global hotspots into insights that can reshape Western military theory and practice. The enemy guerrillas fighting the West in the Middle East, he argues, have in some ways adapted to combat better because of the diversity of their fighters, the intense pressure on them to evolve or die, and the fact that they do not rotate off the battlefield. Militaries "with too high a proportion of elites" (say, the Australian Defence Force primarily fighting a war in Afghanistan with overworked Special Forces) may prove to be maladaptive by increasing casualty rates among its best fighters and denying their talents and experience to the wider force.

Moreover, the tools the West has deployed – airpower, firepower and persistent surveillance – have defined the circumstances to which enemies must adapt, and thus indirectly determined which have thrived and which have demised.

The second part of the book analyses Russian and Chinese adaptions to Western warfare, which Kilcullen terms respectively "liminal warfare" and "conceptual envelopment". This is Kilcullen at his best, his razor-sharp analysis traversing between macro and micro as he considers weapons, orders of battle and military unit dispositions alongside adversary doctrine, politics and strategy to articulate simply how a resurgent China and Russia plan to beat the West. The logic of China's military modernisation has been well profiled elsewhere, but Kilcullen is able to refine, simplify and extend our thinking. He has more to offer here, connecting the insights he has made to the discussion of geostrategy and alliances in Jakub Grygiel and Wess Mitchell's *The Unquiet Frontier*, or to the competitive strategies espoused by Thomas Mahnken.

Limiting the utility of all this analysis is the fraying concept of the Western military, which the author frames as "countries that apply Western military means", including "non-European nations such as Japan, South Korea, and

Taiwan". He acknowledges, briefly, the differences between, for example, the militaries of Australia, Britain and Germany. But these differences seem worthy of further examination when you consider the forward-looking prescriptions he makes for Western military strategy.

In essence, Kilcullen's theory is to "be like Byzantium". The crucial aspect of a Byzantine strategy is to "preserve strength for the long haul", to prepare for a "drawn-out, centuries-long strategic delaying action". Western leaders should accept that their own decline is possible (if not probable), play for time and seek to encourage a more worthy successor to global leadership than crypto-communist China (as the Byzantines did by seeding the Renaissance in Italy).

The West, Kilcullen proposes, should focus on sustainability and resilience for the long term – for example, shifting to cheap and plentiful military technology rather than the lumbering, exquisite weapons programs favoured by mandarins in Canberra and Washington. Innovate, extend thinking beyond the battlefield, train diplomats with skills that let them shift their contribution from military operations to civilian-led initiatives and back. Limit the forward footprint of military basing, study the enemy and consider adapting their utilisation of guerrilla defence tactics (perhaps an idea for Canada and Australia rather than Italy and Spain). There are intriguing notions of China's social credit system as a vulnerability to be exploited by Western agencies, and another idea for countries such as Australia and Japan to invest in their own area defence and aerial denial systems (an echidna-like defence strategy, in Australia's case).

Kilcullen's Byzantine strategy is a grab bag of good ideas, and much of it is already happening. The US Air Force is shifting to more rapid and cheaper production of fighter aircraft; Australia is studying hypersonic missiles of the sort being developed by Russia as well as expanding and upgrading its capacity for defence diplomacy; many countries in the West are rediscovering political warfare and integrating limits on foreign investment into security planning. It is difficult to see how a concrete Byzantine military strategy could be built among disparate Western countries, whose historical unity is being eroded by an absent America. But, as a provocation, "be like Byzantium" offers plenty to cherrypick from.

The Dragons and the Snakes attempts to "put forward a unified theory of how state and non-state threats now overlap and intersect" and to draw lessons from that to inform a new strategy for how the West should compete militarily. Grappling with terrorist groups operating in the valleys of Afghanistan as well as Chinese leaders operating in Zhongnanhai is no easy task. Sometimes this book creaks under the weight of analysing both. But then, that's the burden national security strategists must bear as they think about the long term. Kilcullen hasn't solved the equation, but he has provided Western militaries with a head start.

James Brown

The Jakarta Method: Washington's Anticommunist Crusade and the Mass Murder Program that Shaped Our World
Vincent Bevins
PublicAffairs

In September 2017, a group of elderly victims of the mass violence that occurred in Indonesia in 1965 and 1966 had planned to gather, with their families, to mark the anniversary at the offices of Jakarta's Legal Aid Institute, known as Lembaga Bantuan Hukum Jakarta (LBH). But the event was shut down by police, in response to the angry demands of ultranationalists and Islamist protesters.

The next day, LBH decided defiantly to hold an ad hoc human rights festival at its offices, with music, comedy and art. The radical right-wingers turned up, in large numbers, barricading attendees in the building. Then they turned violent. Witnesses described fragile genocide survivors in their seventies and eighties trapped inside the venue overnight without food or water, as the mob outside yelled, "Eliminate the communists." It was hours before the rioters were dispersed by authorities, with few arrests.

"The events of the past two days represent a deeply troubling new low," wrote LBH's former director Nurkholis Hidayat. "Never before has a discussion – on any theme – at LBH been broken up by state authorities." This was a grim indictment of President Joko "Jokowi" Widodo, given that LBH was established under the military dictatorship of Suharto. Such is the enduring rhetorical power of anti-communism in Indonesia, even in its two-decades-old democracy.

American journalist Vincent Bevins had relocated from São Paulo to Jakarta just months earlier. That night, he received texts from his roommate, who was inside the building, and he posted them to Twitter. Bevins faced "threats and accusations that I was a communist, or even a member of Indonesia's nonexistent Communist Party," he writes in *The Jakarta Method*. "I had become used to receiving exactly these kinds of messages in South America. The similarities were no coincidence."

The Jakarta Method draws compelling links between the mass killings across the Indonesian archipelago in 1965 and 1966, and the US-backed Brazilian military coup of 1964 and subsequent anti-communist violence in Latin America during the Cold War. As a former *Los Angeles Times* correspondent on South America and South-East Asia correspondent for *The Washington Post*, Bevins is well placed to present the shared history of two distant regions. For *The Jakarta Method*, he conducted interviews and consulted archives across continents in English, Indonesian, Spanish and Portuguese.

An estimated 500,000 to one million people were murdered in Indonesia by the army, militias and criminal gangs. A further 1.5 million were imprisoned due to alleged communist connections. These numbers often obscure the individual losses. Bevins does the important work of illuminating the destruction wrought on victims, such as Indonesian couple Francisca and Zain, two of the book's protagonists: "They were sentenced to annihilation, and almost everyone around them was sentenced to a lifetime of guilt, trauma, and being told they had sinned unforgivably because of their association with the earnest hopes of left-wing politics."

Yet as the book shows, the consequences of the mass violence extended beyond the immediate victims. It resulted in the extermination of Indonesia's left – a legacy still felt today in the absence of any serious social democratic party in the nation – and enabled a power grab by Suharto, the "smiling general" once named the world's most corrupt leader ever by *Forbes*. Many figures that served under his New Order regime, such as Luhut Binsar Panjaitan – a former general who now serves as a gatekeeper for Jokowi – remain in positions of influence today.

While Brazil established the National Truth Commission to investigate human rights violations under the Fifth Brazilian Republic military dictatorship, in Indonesia there remains total impunity for state-sanctioned perpetrators of violence under Suharto. There has also been no serious attempt to prosecute the executors of subsequent egregious human rights abuses – such as the abductions and forced disappearances of pro-democracy activists in 1998, allegedly under orders from then special forces commander Prabowo Subianto (now Indonesia's defence minister) and then defence minister Wiranto (now a presidential adviser to Jokowi).

In 2012, Indonesia's national human rights commission released a landmark report on the massacres in 1965–66, which called on the state to establish a truth and reconciliation commission and issue a formal apology to victims. But the report was rejected by the attorney-general. Its findings have never been accepted by the government, nor its recommendations implemented.

That same year, Oscar-nominated documentary *The Act of Killing*, directed by Joshua Oppenheimer, highlighted the massacres to mainstream Western audiences for the first time. Bevins says he hopes his book will be "complementary" to *The Act of Killing* and the 2014 follow-up, *The Look of Silence*, and, rightly, urges readers to watch them.

In 2015, the International People's Tribunal, held in The Hague to investigate "50 years of silence", found Indonesia responsible for crimes against humanity and genocide. Chief Justice Zak Yacoob, a South African jurist and anti-apartheid activist, ruled that ten gross human rights violations had taken place: mass killing, imprisonment, slavery, torture, forced disappearance, sexual violence, banishment, false propaganda, international complicity and genocide.

As Bevins maintains, the United States was not simply a tacit bystander of these crimes. Agents of the nascent CIA were actively involved: "What happened in Brazil in 1964 and Indonesia in 1965 may have been the most important victories of the Cold War for the side that ultimately won – that is, the United States and the global economic system now in operation."

They knew that Indonesia, now the world's fourth most-populous country, was a far more important prize than Vietnam ever could have been. In just a few months, the US foreign policy establishment achieved there what it failed to get done in ten bloody years of war in Indochina.

Declassified documents have shown that Australia, along with America and the United Kingdom, engaged in black propaganda campaigns to whip up anti-communist hysteria, including using Radio Australia to broadcast army propaganda.

Indonesia remains one of the only countries where communism is illegal. This ban is not simply a relic of the past. It is used increasingly today to criminalise activism across Indonesia – particularly when environmentalists seek to get in the way of capitalist exploitation of the country's immense natural resources.

Around the same time that LBH's office was barricaded in 2017, prominent environmental activist Heri Budiawan was arrested at the other end of Java for allegedly displaying communist iconography during a demonstration against a gold mine.

Accused of carrying a banner featuring a hammer and sickle during a protest in Banyuwangi, East Java, Heri was handed a ten-month sentence. He appealed, and it was increased to four years by the Supreme Court. He remains in jail.

Across Indonesia, seizures of leftist literature are commonplace. In July 2019, for instance, police and military raided a literary collective in East Java, seizing books about the head of the defunct Indonesian Communist Party, D.N. Aidit, who was shot by pro-Suharto forces in November 1965. "The spectre of [the Communist Party] did not disappear with the collapse of the New Order," wrote Herlambang P. Wiratraman, a lecturer in human rights at Airlangga University, late last year. "Instead, we are witnessing its return in the courtroom."

As *The Jakarta Method* highlights, the world may well have forgotten about the devastating events of 1965–66, but they have had enduring political consequences for the nation – and, for millions of people, they remain an inescapable part of their daily lives.

Max Walden

Correspondence

"Beijing Calling"
by Michael Wesley

Ashley Townshend

Reshaping the Australia–United States alliance for a contested Indo-Pacific should be at the top of Canberra's strategic policy agenda. In his sweeping essay "Beijing Calling" (AFA8, February 2020), Michael Wesley offers a compelling account of the way that past Australian leaders have renegotiated the alliance at key junctures in our history. He rightly calls for another alliance makeover and an end to the sentimentality about "mateship" that risks obscuring the interests-based calculations at the heart of our entente.

Wesley examines the alliance through the lens of intensifying US–China competition, focusing on how this will test relations between Canberra and Washington. It is a critical question for Australia. But it cannot be answered without a hard-headed assessment of our interests in the alliance as the Indo-Pacific strategic environment deteriorates rapidly. This omission in Wesley's otherwise thoughtful essay leads him to the untenable conclusion that Australia should make the alliance more about diplomacy and development, and less about military matters, at precisely the time we should be deepening our capacity for collective defence with the United States and other partners in the region.

Any debate about the future of the Australia–United States alliance must start with a clear sense of the kind of regional order we want. Alliances, after all, are tools to advance shared interests. Wesley identifies these interests as maintaining "commercial access and political influence" in the region; securing the string of territories often called the First Island Chain, which extends from Japan to Taiwan and down to South-East Asia; and preventing the rise of a "hostile power" that could dominate our neighbourhood.

The achievement of these priorities depends on a regional balance of power that is favourable to us. Canberra and Washington underscore this in their latest foreign policy documents, including Australia's 2017 Foreign Policy White Paper and the Trump administration's 2017 National Security Strategy. We need a region-wide counterweight to China's power to ensure Beijing cannot employ military threats and other forms of leverage to coerce us or our partners with impunity.

The United States has maintained a commanding presence in the Indo-Pacific for the best part of seventy years, underscored by its unrivalled capacity to project military power abroad. But the era of uncontested American primacy is over. As my colleagues and I argued in the United States Studies Centre report "Averting Crisis", a dangerous mix of strategic overstretch, budget dysfunction and underinvestment in high-end military equipment is straining the Pentagon's ability to sustain a favourable balance of power in the region. China, meanwhile, has invested in a formidable array of advanced missiles, fighter jets, submarines and other "counter-intervention" systems in a bid to lock US forces out of the Western Pacific. These dynamics are not only eroding Washington's capacity to deter Chinese aggression along the First Island Chain and arrest its creeping expansion into the South China Sea; they're also emboldening Beijing to use "grey zone" tactics – such as political warfare, influence operations and economic coercion – to incrementally transform the Indo-Pacific in ways that undercut our ability to respond.

Put simply: the strategic order upon which Australia's interests depend is falling apart and can't be salvaged by the United States alone. Although Washington, as Wesley observes, is working to strengthen its regional position and deny Beijing military "supremacy", this will require growing input from US allies and partners. Like-minded nations need to transition from living under the protection of America's increasingly porous security umbrella to contributing actively to a strategy of collective defence in which all play a role in deterring Chinese adventurism.

This should be the focus of our efforts to reshape the Australia–United States alliance, as well as the lodestar by which we advance our regional partnerships. But we have a long way to go. Australia and the United States, despite our close defence ties and high level of interoperability, lack mechanisms for identifying common thresholds for action, coordinating military strategy and undertaking combined contingency planning. Such measures are crucial for transforming the alliance into a credible vehicle for preventing wars, and should proceed in parallel with efforts to bolster military cooperation with Japan, India, Singapore, Indonesia and other capable partners.

None of this will be straightforward. While Canberra and Washington have overlapping visions for the Indo-Pacific order, our individual security interests and threat perceptions regarding China are far from identical. On this, Wesley is right that China "tests the alliance". But this is also why we must update the alliance's capacity for strategic coordination – which is as much about identifying divergences and addressing expectation gaps as it is about readying our armed forces to offset shortfalls in America's regional military presence and bolster our common interests in deterrence.

Some will respond that collective defence is precisely the kind of "military mindset" that Wesley dismisses as myopic. This ignores the fact that regional orders are ultimately founded on the distribution of hard power, even as they're sustained by trade, diplomacy and institutions. All are obviously needed. But it is only by tending to our region's deteriorating balance of power that we can begin to achieve the goal Wesley sets for the Australia–United States alliance: to "convince China's neighbours that is it possible to retain their strategic independence".

Ashley Townshend is director of foreign policy and defence at the University of Sydney's United States Studies Centre.

Elena Collinson

I n tracing the evolution of Australia's loosening of fraternal ties with the United Kingdom during the sunset years of Empire through the genesis of its alliance with the United States to the present, Michael Wesley illustrates the adage in diplomacy that there are no permanent friends, just permanent interests. Further, serving those interests depends on changing geopolitical and economic dynamics.

The thrust of his piece is that "the new challenge of Asia for Australia and the United States is not military but diplomatic and developmental". Arguably, given China's emphasis on defence spending and its increasingly sophisticated militarisation of the South China Sea, including its vigilance in confronting freedom-of-navigation operations in the area, the military imperative of the Australia–US alliance remains as important as ever.

That said, Wesley is right that diplomacy and development assistance ought to be better honed to ensure that China does not achieve unconditional dominance in the Indo-Pacific. War can be averted if the ledger of hearts and minds in the region shows balance. This is where diplomacy and development assistance find their greatest justification: the cultures of countries in the region tend to be largely personal in nature, meaning that weight is placed on the moral obligation to reciprocate, and the concept of *utang na loob* (roughly translated, from Tagalog, as 'debt of gratitude') is deeply ingrained. Wesley's piece, however, raises the question of how Australia can shift its focus to diplomacy – a change that, though necessary, will involve serious challenges.

Australia's aid budget is dismally low, especially compared with other OECD countries, and its diplomatic footprint is undersized, with the Department of Foreign Affairs and Trade experiencing continued operational budget cuts. But simply boosting funding will not ensure a diplomatic and developmental strategy succeeds. Funding must be underpinned by complementary domestic policies to convince our neighbours that we are sincere. Demonstrating, for example, that climate change is being taken seriously might help Australia to present itself as a genuine partner for countries on the frontline of rising sea levels. So too might proactively addressing continued political underrepresentation of ethnic minorities – only 4 per cent of Australian federal MPs have non-European heritage, and the spectre of the White Australia policy endures in the region's memory.

Wesley asserts that Australia may now have greater leverage in its relationship with the United States. But an attempt to recast the alliance towards diplomacy and development at the expense of its military dimension could be hampered by lack of domestic support in some influential policymaking quarters. Alliance management in recent years has been informed by China's growing assertiveness. At the same time, the China debate in Australia has become increasingly toxic, with positioning on the subject taken to denote loyalty to country. So what should be a self-evident and logical approach – adjusting the alliance to ensure it better suits changed circumstances – is clouded by emotion, in addition to resource constraints. Does one put scarce money into butter or guns? In such an environment, hewing out a more sophisticated dimension to alliance diplomacy – especially when the ANZUS Treaty has become a template for the relationship as a whole – is a herculean task.

All this is, of course, not to say that one should shy away from it.

Any discussion of how the alliance might be reshaped should also consider the question of demographics. There are some indications that younger Australians are lukewarm on the alliance. According to the Lowy Institute Poll 2019, support for a strong alliance as an extension of shared values and ideals has been in decline since 2011 across all age groups, but markedly in the 18–29 age bracket. Support in this group dropped from 76 per cent in 2011 to 72 per cent in 2015 to 62 per cent in 2019 – an indication that while the Trump administration may have accelerated the downward trajectory, it is not the sole cause. The United States seems keenly aware of this trend, with its State Department dedicating resources to programs targeting "next-generation alliance managers" in Australia.

That next generation is coming to maturity with a very different view of American global leadership. They see a United States turned inwards and in relative decline. But Canberra elites are struggling to squarely face this changing America, or this evolving demographic outlook at home. They remain rusted on to an older view of the alliance, and keen to respond to the demands of their great-power ally – demands that will surely continue to intensify into the next administration, whether Republican or Democrat. Such a US posture will only intensify Australia's need to restore diplomacy as the primary driver of our international engagement. This will be a challenge, to be sure, but one that needs to be met head-on.

Elena Collinson is a senior researcher in the Australia–China Relations Institute at the University of Technology Sydney.

Michael Wesley responds

Elena Collinson's and Ashley Townshend's responses to "Beijing Calling" offer important points that, taken together, add to my conclusion of just how necessary it is to work to reshape Australia's alliance with the United States. They also suggest – for very different reasons – why it will be a difficult thing for today's Australia to contemplate.

Townshend points out that without "a hard-headed assessment of our interests in the alliance as the Indo-Pacific strategic environment deteriorates rapidly", we cannot hope to think about how to reshape the alliance. He's dead right. Australia's interests are exactly those of any state entering an alliance: to achieve as much security as possible at the lowest cost. Without ANZUS, Australia would have to spend vastly more on its defence than it has done for the past seventy years – and that would mean spending less on schools, hospitals and social security. Put crudely, clever alliance management has helped underpin one of the world's highest standards of living.

And this is where the hard part of Townshend's argument hits. He rightly says that a favourable regional order must rest on a favourable balance of hard military power. But "the strategic order upon which Australia's interests depend is falling apart and can't be salvaged by the United States alone" – meaning Australia, Japan and other countries that have grown wealthy while an uncontested America underwrites their security will need to start investing heavily in their own and the region's military power. The problem is that the combined rate of change in America and its Pacific allies' defence spending continues to see the military balance shifting in China's favour. To change that requires truly massive military spending – orders of magnitude beyond current levels.

That's not a conversation the Australian government seems ready to have with our society.

Luckily, regional order doesn't only consist of guns and ships. It also consists of institutions and perceptions, which are shaped by diplomacy and development. It's in this space that China is making a significant effort because it rightly regards institutions and perceptions as critical to the eventual power structure in Asia. Townshend believes my suggestion that the alliance be used to leverage diplomacy and development is "untenable", but it's precisely because Canberra and Washington have gone to sleep in these areas that Beijing has been given its greatest opportunity to advance its regional ambitions.

To be clear: I'm not arguing for fewer missiles and more diplomats and aid; I'm arguing for more of each. They're a custom set. Instead, we've been investing moderately in weapons while stripping away our diplomatic and development capacity. And here's a secret for cabinet to think about: diplomats and aid are a lot cheaper than weapons systems and soldiers, and their impact can be much more enduring.

Here Collinson makes an intriguing intervention when she brings culture into the equation. She suggests that diplomacy and development need to be carefully thought through and targeted in the region if they are to have the effects we want. The genuineness of a country's commitment to its neighbours has long-term implications for attitudes and the way that institutions are managed. Although she doesn't say it explicitly, Collinson's implication is that Australia will need to shift away from a transactional approach to regional relations if it plans to have these sorts of impacts on its key neighbours – perhaps a major cultural challenge for us right here.

Collinson then raises another crucial point – about the role public opinion plays in shaping the context of Australia's strategic policy. She rightly points out that the debate on China in Australia "has become increasingly toxic", while Australians – particularly younger generations – are growing sceptical about the ideals overlap between Australia and the United States. This is important because energised public opinion can constrain creative foreign policymaking. Baiting Beijing may make sense for the government's focus groups, but it doesn't help prepare the ground for the creative curation of a difficult relationship in future. And creative curation is just what's needed in the regional order that's emerging.

Michael Wesley is deputy vice-chancellor international
at the University of Melbourne.

"Developing a Grand Compact for the Pacific" by John Blaxland

Nic Maclellan

n "The Fix" (AFA8, February 2020), John Blaxland proposes that "Australia should offer a compact of association with South Pacific countries, allowing for shared governance". Such compacts would offer Australian residency and potentially citizenship to individuals from four countries – Kiribati, Tuvalu, Nauru and Tonga – alongside a "similar but less all-encompassing supportive arrangement" for those from larger states such as Vanuatu, Solomon Islands and Fiji.

Blaxland's proposal has fundamental flaws. It underestimates the dynamism of contemporary Pacific regionalism, ignores current debates over security, self-determination and sovereignty in the region, and perpetuates neocolonial values that devalue Pacific culture, identity and agency.

The idea of a compact of free association with Pacific nations is not new. Variations on a security and migration trade-off have previously been floated by economist Ross Garnaut, former prime minister Kevin Rudd and Australian Defence Force Lieutenant Colonel Greg Colton. The idea draws on Howard-era proposals for a Pacific community with an integrated economy and a single currency, the Rudd government's Pacific Partnerships for Development and Security, and the 2017 Foreign Policy White Paper, which aims "to integrate Pacific countries into the Australian and New Zealand economies and our security institutions".

But why is a compact of association required? If the offer of citizenship is sincere, why doesn't Australia – like New Zealand – establish a Pacific access visa category, without demanding a security quid pro quo? The World Bank has already proposed that Australia and New Zealand allow open access to people from Kiribati and Tuvalu, without the need for a compact. We could open up pathways to citizenship for existing Pacific seasonal workers. Beyond this,

Australia might support appropriate relocation to other island nations, rather than to the outer suburbs of Sydney, Brisbane and Auckland.

Blaxland seems reluctant to articulate clearly the key objective of his proposal, which is to maintain Australia's long-standing policy of strategic denial in the Pacific islands. In his 2017 proposal for a compact of free association, published in an article on the Lowy Institute website, the ADF's Greg Colton is more honest – the objective is to contain China's growing influence and reinforce the ANZUS alliance:

> If Australia were to incorporate Nauru, Tuvalu and Kiribati into a compact of free association, it would deny China the ability to become the dominant external influence in these three countries. Looked at on a global map, this would in effect extend and deepen the second island chain formed by the US Free Compact States and enhance Australia's alliance with the US.

Blaxland's focus on Australia's historic Anglophone partners seems quaint and outdated. He asserts: "At the time of Australia's federation, much of the Pacific consisted of British colonies." Well, yes, apart from the Portuguese in Timor; the Germans in New Guinea, Samoa and Micronesia; the French in New Caledonia and the Établissements français de l'Océanie; the Americans in Hawaii, Guam and American Samoa; and the Dutch in the East Indies and Dutch New Guinea.

Migration pathways are a key legacy of this colonialism: people from US Freely Associated States head to Guam, Hawaii and Arkansas; Samoa, Cook Islands, Tokelau and Niue are granted access to New Zealand; the French dependencies are the responsibility of Paris. Blaxland's proposal of compacts for just four countries implicitly accepts this colonial carve-up, but ignores the realities of contemporary migration, labour mobility and transnational networks of kin.

Many Pacific countries today are eager to transcend these historic colonial divisions. Tonga and Tuvalu are active in the Polynesian Leaders Group, alongside American, French and New Zealand territories and other independent Polynesian states. Kiribati and Nauru participate fully alongside US compact states and territories in Micronesian leaders' summits. New Caledonia and French Polynesia are now full members of the Pacific Islands Forum.

Blaxland underestimates the dynamism of this Pacific diplomacy. He also fails to recognise the significance of the Pacific Small Island Developing States (PSIDS) group at the United Nations. PSIDS was created expressly to develop collective diplomacy by island states – without Australia and New Zealand in the room. The Asian bloc at the United Nations now includes the PSIDS group, providing support for Fiji to win the presidency of the UN General Assembly, chair global climate negotiations and co-host the first global oceans summit.

Gaining confidence from more than twenty years of climate diplomacy, PSIDS is now striking out into international negotiations on oceans, fisheries and development finance, as documented in Greg Fry and Sandra Tarte's book *The New Pacific Diplomacy*. While Australia is still a crucial development partner, this increased South–South diplomacy runs counter to the notion that Canberra has the answers to "governance, security, stability and prosperity in the Pacific".

Would Blaxland's "shared governance" require constitutional reform, in line with Kevin Rudd's 2019 suggestion of "a formal constitutional condominium" with three smaller island states? Given the repeated failure to amend the Australian constitution to develop a treaty with Aboriginal and Torres Strait Islander peoples, this notion of pan-Pacific constitutional change seems far-fetched. Under international law on decolonisation, compacts of free association were designed as a step towards sovereignty – why would Tuvalu, Kiribati and especially Tonga go backwards and renounce full control of their territory and ocean? (Oh, to be a fly on the wall when the Australian high commissioner tells the king of Tonga he must share governance with Canberra.)

Blaxland does acknowledge that "it will be critical to articulate the mutual benefits, lest the arrangement appear a neo-colonial land grab". The danger is that the push for shared control of exclusive economic zones will seem a neo-colonial *ocean* grab. At a time of regional debates on sustainable ocean management, many Pacific citizens are concerned about proposals for seabed mining, deep-sea oil and gas exploration, climate geoengineering and the biopiracy of marine life.

Indigenous control of land and ocean resources is more than a matter of "local sensitivities and cultural idiosyncrasies". Many islanders are well aware of the sorry history of Australian attempts to control oil resources in the Timor Sea. They are wary of new ANZUS military bases in the region, including the Australian/US support for an expanded naval facility on Manus Island.

Blaxland recognises that "the success of a free compact arrangement will depend on presenting it in a respectful manner that considers Pacific environmental sensibilities". But the proposed loss of sovereignty is unlikely to be accepted if improved migration to Australia is simply the carrot that allows Canberra to drive foreign policy and deny China strategic influence in the region. A formal compact might also require Australia to choose sides in current maritime boundary claims, such as Tonga's dispute with Fiji over the Minerva Reefs or Vanuatu's dispute with France over Matthew and Hunter islands.

The other fatal flaw of this proposal is the lack of realism about global warming. The climate emergency threatens us all – not just low-lying atoll states. It is already impacting on food and water security across the Mekong, Ganges and Yangtze deltas. If Funafuti and South Tarawa are threatened, so too are Miami, London and other major cities. Last summer's megafires devastated Australian farms, bushland and biodiversity, and Royal Australian Navy vessels were diverted to evacuate citizens off the beach at Mallacoota in Victoria. Blaxland's proposal seems to put off the hard choices on climate action that have paralysed Australian policymakers for two decades and alienated our island neighbours.

Nic Maclellan is a correspondent for Islands Business
magazine (Fiji) and other Pacific media.

Tarcisius Kabutaulaka

John Blaxland's proposal for a "grand compact for the Pacific" is Australia-centric and marginalises Pacific islander voices. It highlights Australia's continuing struggle to define its relationship with the region as well as its concerns about the changing geopolitical order as China's influence grows.

Canberra's fetishisation of and desire to lead the South Pacific is not new. For many Australian politicians, bureaucrats and academics, the region is their "patch" – a place that is simultaneously an exotic tourist destination, a research topic and a strategic sphere of influence. They also view it as an "arc of instability", a sweeping curve of countries marred by poor governance, as journalist Graeme Dobell and others have noted. In this relationship, Australia is characterised variously: as neighbour, enforcer, leader, big brother, development partner. Some even view Australia as a member of the region.

Academic Greg Fry has long critiqued Australia's negative representations of Pacific island countries and its self-aggrandisement as the leader with the solutions to the region's problems – an outlook he reviewed again in his 2019 book, *Framing the Islands*. Ideas of a "compact", in which Australia plays a leadership role, have emerged more recently, for example in proposals by Australian Defence Force Lieutenant Colonel Greg Colton and former Australian prime minister Kevin Rudd.

Blaxland's plan continues Australia's quest to define its role in and relationship to the region. This proposal comes with an offer of residency (and potentially citizenship) for Pacific islanders "should the situation become untenable in their home islands". It also offers shared governance and surveillance of territorial and maritime domains. These elements might be attractive to some South Pacific countries. In February 2020, Kiribati's former president Anote Tong told ABC News that Blaxland's proposal would be difficult for small island countries to turn down. However, it is unlikely that Pacific leaders will accept the proposal if it means giving up their sovereignty. Given the region's long history of colonialism and exploitation, sovereignty is these countries' bastion of dignity.

Climate change is central to this discussion. Blaxland states that the compact must consider "Pacific environmental sensibilities". Herein lies Australia's blind spot. Climate change is exposing not only the vulnerability of island nations, but also the responsibility of countries such as Australia to reduce carbon emissions. A compact must address "the risks of environmental disaster" as well as its causes. The eighteen-member Pacific Islands Forum, which includes Australia, identifies climate change as the most important existential threat to the islands. The Kainaki II Declaration, a document that emerged from the PIF, recognises the "climate change crisis" and makes an appeal for urgent action. Yet the Australian government repeatedly defies such calls, indicating that it is part of the problem. Canberra must change its climate policies before it reaches out to island countries for a compact of association, otherwise this will be seen as a way to excuse itself from reducing its carbon footprint.

Blaxland proposes an arrangement similar to the Compact of Free Association (COFA) that the United States has with Palau, the Federated States of Micronesia and the Marshall Islands, which allows citizens of these countries US immigration access and financial assistance. In return, the United States reserves the right to use these places for military purposes. But COFA is far from fair. Migrants from these countries are not offered the same benefits as US citizens and nationals. Perhaps New Zealand's arrangements with the Cook Islands and Niue offer a better model, since they grant NZ citizenship.

Underlying Blaxland's proposal is the need to "protect Australia's long-term interests in the Pacific" in light of China's growing influence. But Australia must respect island countries' rights to choose their diplomatic partners. China is here to stay and provides an attractive alternative to Western dominance. It is a major trading partner to, and a source of much-needed assistance for, some island countries. Australia must accept that the new regional order includes

China. There is, however, credence in Canberra's concern that Beijing's concessional loans could leave island countries indebted.

Although certain aspects of Blaxland's proposal might appeal to some Pacific leaders, for any compact to work Australia must be clear about the nature of its relationship with Pacific island countries. It must be prepared to genuinely listen to and respect the sovereignty of these ocean states.

Associate Professor Tarcisius Kabutaulaka is the director of the Center for Pacific Islands Studies at the University of Hawai'i at Mānoa.

John Blaxland responds

Thank you to Nic Maclellan and Tarcisius Kabutaulaka for the comments on my article. I am pleased for the opportunity to reply.

Maclellan's summary of my proposal in "The Fix" oversimplifies and unfortunately dismisses it with some superlatives. My article proposes the development of a comprehensive approach to Australia's relations with select South Pacific countries. It is addressed principally at states that share a strong heritage with Australia, based on common law and use of the English language – and even then, the priority is on the four most vulnerable micro states, Kiribati, Tonga, Tuvalu and Nauru. It deliberately avoids discussion of other parts of the neighbourhood where Dutch, Portuguese and French influences colour perceptions.

Maclellan claims that the proposal "underestimates" current debates over issues such as security in the South Pacific region. The purpose of "The Fix" is not to provide a tour d'horizon or analysis of all contentious issues. I was not given the word count for that. Instead, the intention is to propose a positive, workable solution to these problems. My article sets out a practical, mutually beneficial answer to regional concerns about security, climate change and other governance-related issues.

As for the assertion that the proposal "perpetuates neo-colonial values", I find this unhelpful and misleading – it caricatures the notion of a compact of association, which is intended to ensure mutual benefit, not one-sided exploitation. My article stresses the need for visionary and respectful Australian engagement. The proposal is about *shared* governance and *mutually beneficial* partnership, not some gratuitous power grab.

Maclellan goes on to suggest more limited alternatives to a compact, such as a Pacific access visa category. Such ideas have been floated before, but offer insufficient incentive for Australian political leaders to take them seriously. There has to be something of value in the concept for Australian politicians to see it as sellable to the Australian voting public, which includes an element that is afraid of opening the doors too widely. I am suggesting we develop a grand compact for the Pacific because lesser approaches do not go far enough to meet either the needs of Pacific island states or the Australian expectation that it will benefit from making an offer on the scale of generosity that I have outlined.

Maclellan says the "key objective" of the proposal is to maintain strategic denial in the Pacific islands. This is an unhelpful, reductionist interpretation of a multipronged proposal. My article makes the point that Chinese loans give China influence over small island communities; this is undeniable. But combatting China's influence is not the main rationale for my proposal. China lends to Australia as well. But China's loans have led to governance concerns in the smallest of Pacific island states, and Australia has the ability to offer a greater helping hand on this issue.

My article outlines a balanced compact for the Pacific on a scale that has not been considered seriously before. This is because the problems we face are now greater, more complicated and more intertwined. Such an overture would not discount Pacific islands' right to choose whether to accept it. They may or may not select Australia as a migration destination. They may or may not take up the offer of shared governance. But as climate-related challenges mount, the proposal may become increasingly attractive. And by putting it forward for consideration, Australia could potentially improve its relations with the states of the Pacific – and even perhaps overcome some of its hang-ups about climate change.

The response from Tarcisius Kabutaulaka recalls that Anote Tong, Kiribati's former president, told the ABC in February 2020 that a grand compact of association would be difficult for small island countries to turn down. Yet in a leap of unexplained reasoning, Kabutaulaka goes on to say it is unlikely that Pacific leaders would accept if it meant giving up their sovereignty. A closer reading of my article would dispel this view. It does not propose that Pacific island nations – or Australia – give up sovereignty.

Let's be clear. The proposal is being put forward by an Australian citizen, not a government entity or a politician, and it does not seek to marginalise Pacific islander voices. Besides, what difference does it make who proposes the idea? If it is feasible and attractive, as Tong suggests, what is there to object to? By its nature, a proposal can be accepted or turned down.

Others are welcome to make suggestions to change and improve the idea of a compact of association. I would ask, however, that my proposal be read as it was intended: made in good faith as a practical response to the challenges facing us all, Australian and Pacific islander, today. It would be mutually beneficial, offering Pacific island citizens shared governance, and Australian residence and migration if required.

Both respondents' concerns about climate change are well made. As this past summer's Australian bushfires demonstrated yet again, climate change is impinging on us all and we should confront it together. Clearly, much more needs to be done, but this problem cannot be solved overnight and Australian politicians need some persuading as well. The offers of Australian residency and citizenship, and shared governance, should be seen in this spirit. The threats faced by some Pacific island states are becoming too urgent and existential to procrastinate. Shunning the idea of a grand compact of association won't help.

As Kabutaulaka says, Australia must be prepared to genuinely listen to and respect the sovereignty of these ocean states. Equally, I hope that readers in Pacific island states will consider the proposal with an open mind and see its potential. The same must be true of Australian government officials in Canberra. With that approach, we stand a chance of fixing this together.

John Blaxland is a professor of security and intelligence studies at the Strategic and Defence Studies Centre at the Australian National University.

Subscribe to Australian Foreign Affairs & save up to 28% on the cover price.

Enjoy free home delivery of the print edition and full digital as well as ebook access to the journal via the Australian Foreign Affairs website, iPad, iPhone and Android apps.

Forthcoming issue:
Friends, Allies and Enemies
(October 2020)

Never miss an issue. Subscribe and save.

☐ **1 year auto-renewing print and digital subscription** (3 issues) $49.99 within Australia. Outside Australia $79.99*.

☐ **1 year print and digital subscription** (3 issues) $59.99 within Australia. Outside Australia $99.99.

☐ **1 year auto-renewing digital subscription** (3 issues) $29.99.*

☐ **2 year print and digital subscription** (6 issues) $114.99 within Australia.

☐ Tick here to commence subscription with the current issue.

Give an inspired gift. Subscribe a friend.

☐ **1 year print and digital gift subscription** (3 issues) $59.99 within Australia. Outside Australia $99.99.

☐ **1 year digital-only gift subscription** (3 issues) $29.99.

☐ **2 year print and digital gift subscription** (6 issues) $114.99 within Australia.

☐ Tick here to commence subscription with the current issue.

ALL PRICES INCLUDE GST, POSTAGE AND HANDLING.

*Your subscription will automatically renew until you notify us to stop. Prior to the end of your subscription period, we will send you a reminder notice.

Please turn over for subscription order form, or subscribe online at **australianforeignaffairs.com**
Alternatively, call 1800 077 514 or +61 3 9486 0288 or email **subscribe@australianforeignaffairs.com**

Back Issues

ALL PRICES INCLUDE GST, POSTAGE AND HANDLING.

☐ **AFA1** ($15.99)
The Big Picture

☐ **AFA2** ($15.99)
Trump in Asia

☐ **AFA3** ($15.99)
Australia & Indonesia

☐ **AFA4** ($15.99)
Defending Australia

☐ **AFA5** ($15.99)
Are We Asian Yet?

☐ **AFA6** ($15.99)
Our Sphere of Influence

☐ **AFA7** ($22.99)
China Dependence

☐ **AFA8** ($22.99)
Can We Trust America?

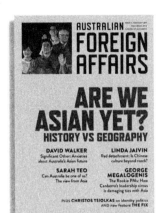

PAYMENT DETAILS I enclose a cheque/money order made out to Schwartz Books Pty Ltd. Or please debit my credit card (MasterCard, Visa or Amex accepted).

CARD NO. ☐☐☐☐ ☐☐☐☐ ☐☐☐☐ ☐☐☐☐

EXPIRY DATE   /   CCV   AMOUNT $

CARDHOLDER'S NAME

SIGNATURE

NAME

ADDRESS

EMAIL   PHONE

Post or fax this form to: Reply Paid 90094, Carlton VIC 3053 **Freecall:** 1800 077 514 **or** +61 3 9486 0288
Fax: (03) 9011 6106 **Email:** subscribe@australianforeignaffairs.com **Website:** australianforeignaffairs.com
Subscribe online at australianforeignaffairs.com/subscribe (please do not send electronic scans of this form)

The Back Page

DIPLOMATIC FLU

What is it: Any malady feigned to avoid an awkward political situation; also called diplomatic illness. It is unrelated to diplomatic immunity.

Who has had it: Boris Yeltsin (former president, Russia) had repeated bouts of mystery "heart trouble" that absented him from several tense events. Critics blamed diplomatic flu; others believed it was genuine ill health caused by heavy drinking. Henry Kissinger (diplomat, United States) caught diplomatic flu in Pakistan in 1971 and secretly travelled to China ahead of a visit by Richard Nixon.

Who hasn't: Allen West (former Republican congressman, Florida) accused Hillary Clinton (former secretary of state, United States) of having "Benghazi flu" when she cancelled a Capitol Hill hearing due to a concussion. She later presented medical evidence of the injury.

Who had the worst case: Due to appear at the closing ceremony of the 1962 Seattle World's Fair, John F. Kennedy (former president, United States) cancelled with a sniffle. The "cold" was the Cuban Missile Crisis.

When was the first outbreak: In England, "diplomatic gout" dates back to at least the sixteenth century. Lorenzo Campeggio (last cardinal protector, England) came down with it on his way to meet Cardinal Wolsey (statesman, England) when King Henry VIII announced his divorce.

The real thing: Woodrow Wilson (former president, United States) contracted Spanish flu in 1919 at the signing of the Treaty of Versailles. Donald Trump (president, United States) insisted a G7 summit in 2020 be in Washington. Angela Merkel (chancellor, Germany) refused to attend due to the health risk of COVID-19. The summit was rescheduled.